Palgrave Studies in Life Writing

This series features books that address key concepts and subjects, with an emphasis on new and emergent approaches. It offers specialist but accessible studies of contemporary and historical topics, with a focus on connecting life writing to themes with cross-disciplinary appeal. The series aims to be the place to go to for current and fresh research for scholars and students looking for clear and original discussion of specific subjects and forms; it is also a home for experimental approaches that take creative risks with potent materials.

The term 'Life Writing' is taken broadly so as to reflect the academic, public and global reach of life writing, and to continue its democratic tradition. The series seeks contributions that address contexts beyond traditional territories – for instance, in the Middle East, Africa and Asia. It also aims to publish volumes addressing topics of general interest (such as food, drink, sport, gardening) with which life writing scholarship can engage in lively and original ways, as well as to further the political engagement of life writing especially in relation to human rights, migration, trauma and repression, sadly also persistently topical themes. The series looks for work that challenges and extends how life writing is understood and practised, especially in a world of rapidly changing digital media; that deepens and diversifies knowledge and perspectives on the subject, and which contributes to the intellectual excitement and the world relevance of life writing.

More information about this series at
http://www.palgrave.com/gp/series/15200

Ana Belén Martínez García

New Forms of Self-Narration

Young Women, Life Writing and Human Rights

palgrave
macmillan

Ana Belén Martínez García
University of Navarra
Pamplona, Navarra, Spain

Palgrave Studies in Life Writing
ISBN 978-3-030-46419-6 ISBN 978-3-030-46420-2 (eBook)
https://doi.org/10.1007/978-3-030-46420-2

This Palgrave Macmillan imprint is published by the registered company Springer Nature Switzerland AG
The registered company address is: Gewerbestrasse 11, 6330 Cham, Switzerland

Acknowledgments

This book was largely written in 2019, thanks to the Spanish Ministry of Education and Universities, through a Modality B Mobility aid for young doctors abroad *José Castillejo* which funded a Visiting Research Fellowship at the Centre for Life-Writing Research (CLWR), at King's College London (UK), January–June 2019. Ref. No. CAS18/00158. I thank my faculty and the Institute for Culture and Society (ICS) at the University of Navarra (Spain), the Spanish government, and Clare and Max, co-directors of the Centre, for their support.

I presented a short version of Chapter 1's introductory section on ethics at the Working with Testimonial Narratives Roundtable at the Writing Activism Early Career Workshop organized by the Oxford Research Centre in the Humanities (TORCH) and the Oxford Centre for Life-Writing (OCLW) at the University of Oxford on February 26, 2019. An earlier version of the section on "bridging the online/offline divide" was presented at the International Auto/Biography Association (IABA)-Europe Conference held in Madrid in June 2019. I am grateful to all those in attendance for their feedback at an early stage of this project. I am also grateful to the editors of the *Journal of English Studies* for permission to reproduce part of my article "Empathy for Social Justice: The Case of Malala Yousafzai" which was previously published in their vol. 17 (2019c): 253–275, https://doi.org/10.18172/jes.3540.

Chapter 2 builds on a previously published original article entitled "Construction and Collaboration in Life-Writing Projects: Malala

Yousafzai's Activist 'I'" (Martínez García 2019a) in the *Journal of Writing in Creative Practice* 12 (1–2): 201–217. I thank the editors for permission to reproduce some of it here. I also thank CLWR at KCL for hosting me as a Visiting Research Fellow at the time of writing. I thank my faculty, ISSA—School of Management Assistants, who believed in my project and kindly funded my first six-month postdoctoral research stay January–June 2017.

An earlier comparison between Malala Yousafzai and Rigoberta Menchú's testimonial narratives was published as a chapter entitled "Narrative Emotions and Human Rights Life Writing" (Martínez García 2016) in the volume *On the Move: Glancing Backwards to Build a Future in English Studies* edited by Aitor Ibarrola-Armendariz and Jon Ortiz de Urbina Arruabarrena. Bilbao: University of Deusto, pp. 127–132. ISBN: 978-84-15759-87-4. Accepted 2 March 2016. Published 17 June 2016. I thank the editors, members of the Spanish Association for Anglo-American Studies (AEDEAN) for their support, and my colleagues at the Panel on Critical Theory for their encouragement.

Parts of Chapters 3 and 4 have been expanded and updated from previous publications: "Unearthing the Past: Bringing Ideological Indoctrination to Light in North Korean Girls' Memoirs," *a/b: Auto/Biography Studies* 32 (3): 587–602 (Martínez García 2017a); "Denouncing Human Trafficking in China: North Korean Women's Memoirs as Evidence," *State Crime Journal* 8 (1): 59–79 (2019b); "TED Talks as Life Writing: Online and Offline Activism," *Life Writing* 15 (4): 487–503 (2018). I thank the copyright holders, The Autobiography Society, Pluto Journals, and Taylor & Francis, respectively, for permission to reproduce.

Chapter 5 has been expanded and updated from an article published in *Prose Studies* (2017b) © 2018 Informa UK Limited, trading as Taylor & Francis Group, available online: https://doi.org/10.1080/01440357.2018.1549310.

Chapter 6 builds on two paper presentations at international venues where I had the pleasure to be a guest speaker: "Refugees' Mediated Testimony: TED Talks" at the Culture and Its Uses as Testimony: Interdisciplinary Approaches Conference, University of Birmingham (UK), 11–12 April 2018, and "Written vs Audiovisual Testimony: Narrating the Migrant Self" presented at the International Workshop on Erratic Bodies, Transitional Borders, and Recent Migration in Europe: Representation and Identity Negotiations in Public Discourse, Literature, and the Arts,

University of Oslo, ILOS, Norway, 27–28 September 2018. I am grateful to the organizers and all those in attendance who gave insightful feedback. Related publications are forthcoming.

A draft of Chapters 7 and 8 was presented at IABA 2019. I thank Sidonie Smith and Julia Watson for encouraging and inspiring a new generation of life-writing scholars.

Contents

CHAPTER 1

Introduction: Life Writing, Human Rights, and Young Women

Abstract This introduction provides an overview of the critical work published over the last few decades on testimonial life writing and women, exploring the conjunction between human rights fights and young women whose role may be considered transgressive in their societies and perhaps signal the rise of transnational feminism. This book is the first-ever attempt at reading side by side life-writing projects of current key icons of human rights activism from the Global South. What brings these case studies together is their strategic use of narrative, English as lingua franca, online/offline methods, and empathy to generate acute social awareness. Each chapter looks at the intriguing ways these activists write themselves, thereby righting the wrongs committed against them, reframing their story as that of an empowered survivor.

Keywords Testimonial life writing · Young women · Human rights activism · Global South · Narrative strategies · Reframing

This book explores life writing by human rights activists who came to prominence in the 2010s. It tracks how certain texts have captured the imagination of contemporary culture, while at the same time serving to advance social justice causes at both a national level and a transnational level. Why are some stories echoed in subsequent humanitarian narratives while some others are left out? Why do some activists become icons while

A. B. Martínez García, *New Forms of Self-Narration*, Palgrave Studies in Life Writing, https://doi.org/10.1007/978-3-030-46420-2_1

some others fall out of sight and/or out of favor? At a time of post-truth, why do we seek authentic reliable sources? How do we navigate the tensions inherent in witnessing these narratives? What are the conditionings for a witness to be believed by the general public? Are there differences across borders, or is there a particular way human rights fights are conveyed? New forms of communication—and therefore of narrating the self—have emerged thanks to the Web 2.0 and the affordances of social media platforms.[1] This book looks at these new forms not as alternative but as complementary methods to more traditional means—such as memoirs and documentaries—allowing publics to engage in advocacy. Human rights, in particular, has benefited greatly from the visibility gained by activists online and offline over the past decades. Wide dissemination and immediacy are key affordances of the digital realm granting access to users worldwide and in real time. Importantly, this arguably less mediated panorama entails opportunities for disadvantaged individuals to empower themselves.[2]

New Forms of Self-Narration is a timely study of young women's life writing as a form of human rights activism. It focuses on six young women who suffered human rights violations when they were girls and have gone on to become activists through life writing. Their ongoing life-writing projects diverge to some extent, but they all coincide in several notable features: They claim a testimonial collective voice, they deploy rights discourse, they excite humanitarian emotions, they link up their context-bound plight with bigger social justice causes, and they use English as their vehicle of self-expression and self-construction. This strategic use of English is of vital importance, as it has brought them together as icons in the public sphere in the last decade. The following young women's life-writing projects are discussed in the present volume: Malala Yousafzai, 2014 Nobel Peace Prize winner who symbolizes the struggle for girls' right to education and for the rights of the displaced; Hyeonseo Lee and Yeonmi Park, two North Korean activists who escaped their country and speak of injustices committed by the Kim regime as well as of the trauma experienced in China and various other countries; Bana Alabed and Nujeen Mustafa, two Syrian refugees who epitomize the Syrian conflict from two opposed angles—endangered child turned youngest Anne Frank phenomenon on Twitter vs disabled teenager turned uneasy spokesperson for refugees; and 2018 Nobel Peace Prize recipient, Nadia Murad, held captive by ISIS in Iraq, now an activist against human trafficking and for ethnic rights. From a position of victimhood, these young women choose to reclaim their identity and, in so doing, rewrite who they are. This is the first-ever attempt to explore all these activists' life-writing texts side by side, encompassing both the written and the audiovisual material, online and offline, and taking all texts as belonging to a unique, single, though multifaceted, project.[3] Though the path has been laid for these investigations in life-writing research, there remain gaps in what we know about testimonial narratives from the Global South and how they may have influenced policies or had repercussions on an international scale. What are the narrative devices deployed by these life writers? How are emotions conveyed, animated, and augmented? What role does mediation play in the shaping of the narrative? What is the relationship between the online and offline realms in these cases? In this book, I argue that the online/offline divide has not only become blurred over time, but that it is necessarily so.

This book will add to the growing number of publications in the field of life writing devoted to how it can work in gaining insight into current conflicts and contributing to a dialogue that might help ethical outcomes. Inspired by scholarly work in testimonial life writing (see Schaffer and Smith 2004; Smith and Watson 2010, 2012, 2017; Whitlock 2007, 2015; Gilmore 2001, 2017a, b; Douglas and Poletti 2016), I draw on life-writing theory to shed light on the aforementioned case studies. By analyzing the narrative strategies these young women use, I hope to offer some clues that may unpack the global phenomenon they pose.

Kay Schaffer and Sidonie Smith's (2004) seminal work, *Human Rights and Narrated Lives: The Ethics of Recognition*, remains influential in subsequent publications on testimonial narratives. Scholars of life writing are now and again drawn to how the authors present human rights life narratives and their analysis of the discursive frames that help reach wide audiences. Their case studies are geographically and culturally diverse: from the South African TRC to the Stolen Generations in Australia, Korean comfort women during World War II, US prison inmates, to Tiananmen Square narratives. Not only do Schaffer and Smith discuss the productive ways in which life narratives fight for social justice, but they also present the pitfalls they may come across, such that the narratives may become complicit in political propaganda struggles or pressures of the literary market. Along the transnational pathways these stories navigate, they may become relocated and affectively charged in new ways. Schaffer and Smith's eloquent explanation of both the difficulties and the possibilities these narratives present has been a source of inspiration for the present book.

Sidonie Smith and Julia Watson's decades-long collaboration continues to inspire life-writing scholars who are drawn to their many publications—either as single authors or together—as well as their constructive criticism at IABA conferences. Attempting to summarize all their work might be too big an undertaking, particularly when they did it so well in their introduction to *Life Writing in the Long Run* (2017). In brief, one might argue their theories on women's self-presentation across diverse times and modes, is of uppermost importance. They have applied a feminist lens to reading women's auto/biographical practices, editing several collections (see 1992, 1996, 1998, 2002). *Interfaces* is a particularly key text as Smith and Watson (2002) develop what they term "visual/verbal interface" (37), an intriguing notion that will permeate this volume as I aim to shed light on the intricate, relevant nature of the relation between image and text in/for young women's life-writing projects. Smith's (2006) work on *Zlata's Diary* has also served as inspiration for the study of young women's narratives of ethnic suffering contained herein. Finally, Smith and Watson's co-authored book (2010) *Reading Autobiography: A Guide to Interpreting Life Narratives* continues to offer clues for the study of all things auto/biographical and can be actually read as a handbook.

Gillian Whitlock (2007) has studied the commodification and circulation of Arab and Muslim women's narratives along the "transit lane" allowing trauma stories to travel rapidly from East to West, from South to North (118). While she acknowledges the value of bringing transgressions to light, she cautions against reductionism and considers some narrative uptakes as a potential "soft weapon" of neoliberalism, "easily co-opted into propaganda" (3). In *Postcolonial Life Narratives: Testimonial Transactions*, moreover, Whitlock addresses "the ebb and flow of social activism and resistance" (6) in which the "first-person account of suffering" (2015, 16) or of "victimization" (76) typical of humanitarian enterprises is embedded. She provides a thorough historical study of such life writing, starting with slave narratives in the eighteenth and nineteenth centuries and exploring how the metaphor of "passages" (73) sticks to later testimonial accounts such as the TRC alongside Antjie Krog's memoirs and those by the Australian Stolen Generations; rape warfare, using the example of Dian Fossey's representation as "gorilla girl" (117) in contrast with silenced violence against women during the armed conflict in the Democratic Republic of Congo; and more contemporary refugee narratives mentioning Edwidge Danticat's auto/biographical recollections of how her uncle was treated in applying for asylum in the United States. Whitlock finishes by stressing the danger of homogenizing all refugees and their plights into a single understandable narrative that fits an established pattern that will grant asylum ideally in the country of their choice. Showcasing examples of how trauma evades representation throughout history, and how there is a growing market for these types of narratives, she warns of the ethical problems these works present with their potential commodification for both the authors themselves and activists in general, while acknowledging that the goal they seek is relevant and much needed.

Leigh Gilmore (2001) has addressed what she calls "limit-cases" (14) of autobiography at the junction of trauma and testimony. With a special focus on gender and relying on Judith Butler's theory of "grievability" (2004, 2009), Gilmore (2017b) summarizes her thoughts on testimony as follows: "A focus on testimony—those verbal acts in which a person bears witness to harm in a public forum—enables us to see how histories of harm and first-person witness intertwine and why their co-construction is so crucial to parsing life narrative" (307). Gilmore's (2017a) reading of the problematics surrounding women's testimony, with growing numbers of supporters and detractors, exemplifies one of the many paradoxes attaching to human rights life writing: "What accounts for the simultaneous popularity and denunciation of this form of testimony?" (83). She has recently co-authored *Witnessing Girlhood* (Gilmore and Marshall 2019) where intersectionality is the chosen critical lens to read girls' testimonial texts.

Kate Douglas's (2010) *Contesting Childhood: Autobiography, Trauma and Memory* paved the way to studies on the representation of children in auto/biographical narratives and their sociopolitical impact (7). Drawing on the feminist motto that "the personal is political" she concludes that, in the case of autobiographies of childhood, this is "inevitably" so (6). Though more intent on exploring adult authors looking back on their pasts, Douglas's comments can be extended to youth, as she has gone on to note elsewhere (Douglas 2015; Douglas and Cardell 2015). In *Life Narratives and Youth Culture: Representation, Agency and Participation,* Kate Douglas and Anna Poletti (2016) explore how young people use new media as a means of self-representation. In so doing, the book is inscribed in life-writing scholarship and moves toward what many see as the current trend in life writing—the digital paradigm—and how it opens possibilities for previously silent or silenced subjects to become agents. Drawing from childhood and youth studies, the book is also highly reliant on sociology in what the authors deem an attempt to overcome stereotypes of young people as passive subjects who let others define their identities. Douglas and Poletti provide several case studies where they highlight the role these life narrators have had in shaping an already long-standing tradition within the field of life writing: young African American life writers, war diarists, child soldier memoirists, the Riot Grrrl, traumatized girlhoods, zine culture, and online activists. Among the many examples they discuss, one may find the case of Malala Yousafzai, which is in fact the following chapter in this volume (Chapter 2). Douglas and Poletti (2016) alert that "spectacular" rather than "everyday" youth (30) usually attract media attention, which means that, in the case of rights transgressions, other disadvantaged individuals that are not that "spectacular" may remain unknown, their plights unheard of. Though aware this is a potential drawback in my analysis, as I deal with highly mediatized case studies, this book asserts the ethical work and awareness-raising the human rights life-writing projects here discussed do. Their "spectacular rhetorics" (Hesford 2011), in which humanitarian narratives are typically steeped, may be redeemed to do some vital work provided certain conditions are met, as will be seen below.

In this book, I am particularly keen on exploring the conjunction between human rights fights and young women whose activism and advocacy may be considered transgressive in their societies and perhaps signal the rise of transnational feminism. To do that, these young women traverse self-narrating paths that make use of and excite distinctive "narrative emotions" (Martínez García 2016).

The Testimonial "I" and the Eye-Witnessing Account

A key factor in choosing the case studies for this book was the fact that these young women endured human rights violations at a very young age. The narrating "I" is therefore both "I-witness" and "eye-witness" (Smith and Watson 2017), in line with many famous testimonial accounts before them, but an interesting feature in the case of the young women this book examines is how they use English to write themselves, instead of—or in combination with—other languages, to testify against those transgressions. Though there may be a collaborator in all these narratives—be that an editor, a co-author, an activist, a parent—the fact remains that these young women are able to speak for themselves in their own words and their own terms when the time comes.

While discussing the "I" of the testimonial witness, another key concept Smith and Watson (2012) develop is that of "metrics of authenticity" as they argue against the tendency to read testimony for verification: "ethical reading practices need not be based primarily on verifying claims of authenticity" (618). Subject of public controversies, the young women in this volume and their stories hark back to Rigoberta Menchú's *testimonio* and similar ones, where the threat of being read as a hoax fills the air. As will be seen next, such accusations, though inevitably attaching to testimonial practices, should not be taken at face value.

The narrating "I" tells the story of the activist, but also that of a bigger community of oppressed people, due to gender, religion, ethnicity, politics, armed conflict, and so on. The case studies I consider here "invariably contend that theirs is an individual voice that stands for a collective self (Martínez García 2017a, 596). Far from being mutually exclusive, these modes of narration can be combined. Taking Rigoberta Menchú's (1984) *testimonio*—and the genre itself (Beverley 1987)—as an example of the productive tension between the "I" of the individual and the "I"—or the "we"—of the community, I follow Schaffer and Smith (2004) in reclaiming the value of such controversial life narratives which, though proved to be somewhat lacking in factual truth (Stoll 1999), are instead full of ethical value and may inspire their and subsequent generations. Thus, Menchú's testimonial narrative endured and prospered, as did the activist and her cause. This has been asserted not only by former detractors (see Stoll 2001) but also by Menchú's (2020) own public role in the twenty-first century. As a Nobel Peace Prize recipient, she effectively inaugurated the movement for indigenous people's rights not only at a national level—in Guatemala—but also at a transnational level. Her iconicity is paradigmatic of young women's testimonial narratives, their faces recognizable across different locales and times. Their "I" is "both individual and collective" (Martínez García 2017a, 588). Indeed, Smith and Watson (2012) had observed how testimonies deploy a narrating "I" that stands for a collective plight (600). When applied to young women's testimonial accounts, this "deployment of an 'I' that is at once individual but also collective is central to understanding [their] message and the endurance [their] testimonial voice may have" (Martínez García 2019a, 213).[4] Thus, through their self-presentation acts the young women activists in this book represent a collective of endangered others, be that Pakistani Swati girls in the case of Malala Yousafzai; North Korean famine-stricken, indoctrinated, trafficked girls in the case of Hyeonseo Lee and Yeonmi Park; Syrian victims of war turned refugees in the case of Bana Alabed and Nujeen Mustafa; and Yazidi survivors of Islamic State terror and sexual slavery in the case of Nadia Murad. Importantly, their identity is made up of these two strands—individual and collective—sometimes at odds, but intricately enmeshed.

The Ethics of Human Rights Life Writing

Back in 2004, two books were published on the complex relationship between ethics and life writing, namely G. Thomas Couser's (2004) *Vulnerable Subjects: Ethics and Life Writing* and Paul John Eakin's (2004) *The Ethics of Life Writing*. They present a different picture of the tensions at the heart of life writing as a method: On the one hand, subjects may be deprived of a voice in instances where someone, though starting out with their best intention, is trying to make their story heard (Couser 2004); on the other hand, Eakin (2004) compiles in his edited collection essays by different scholars interested in the potentials and problematics of life writing. Ethically, life writers navigate the tensions between telling the truth and oversharing, between privacy and public (self-)disclosure. Ethically, too, readers must respond accordingly (14). Eakin (2004, 24) quotes from Richard Kearney (1996) to further explain the moral duty of readers of testimony:

> Certain injustices appeal to narrative imagination to plead their case lest they slip irrevocably into oblivion. Ethical experiences of good and evil, as Nussbaum says, need to be felt upon the pulse of shared emotions. Or as Ricoeur says, commenting on narratives of the Holocaust, the horrible must strike the audience as horrible. It must provoke us to *identify* and empathize with the victims. (43)

Empathy may then lead to changing people's views: "eyewitness testimony has the ability to elicit a passionate, engaged response" (Eakin 2004, 24–25). Over 15 years later, we—early career researchers, scholars, students, activists, practitioners, the general public—still ask ourselves much the same questions: What are the ethical implications of life writing, for those who write it and those who are readers/audience?

Schaffer and Smith (2004) analyze the links between collectivizing plights and rights advocacy:

> These acts of remembering ... issue an ethical call to listeners ... They issue a call within and beyond UN protocols and mechanisms for institutions, communities, and individuals to respond to the story; to recognize the humanity of the teller and the justice of the claim; to take responsibility for that recognition; and to find means of redress. In the specific locales of rights violations and in the larger court of public opinion, life narrative becomes essential to affect recourse, mobilize action, forge communities of interest, and enable social change. (3)

Attending to the expected characteristics of testimonial narratives, they admit that, though problematic, such framing might be positive as well (17). In a way, victimhood and agency seem to be irreversibly entwined in human rights life writing.

Smith and Watson focus, on their co-written articles and books, on the relationship between the narrating "I" and ethics, but are most intent in finding out how exactly women can use life writing to their advantage, as a means of feminist advocacy and activism. In *Reading Autobiography: A Guide for Interpreting Life Narratives*, Smith and Watson (2010) explore the ethics of vulnerability by reading Judith Butler's (2005) *Giving an Account of Oneself* closely. The self "must employ storytelling modes, tropes, and self-positionings to tell about itself ... For Butler, recognizing the self's founding vulnerability is precisely what grounds the ethics of self-accounting (64)" (Smith and Watson 2010, 217). Among those tropes, the girl in need of help of humanitarianism stands out, with many current activists aiming to be read as the new Anne Frank (see Smith 2006; Martínez García 2017b, 2019a).

Whitlock has turned her attention to postcolonial life writing, and to the ethics of appropriating humanitarian tropes and repurposing them to suit activists' needs. In *Soft Weapons: Autobiography in Transit*, she reminds readers that not all testimony can "guarantee the ethical and political conditions that secure an appropriate response: empathic witnessing" (2007, 77). In *Postcolonial Life Narratives: Testimonial Transactions*, she refers to testimonial texts as "texts on the move in search of witnessing publics" (2015, 169). Without others recognizing that suffering and acting as "its witness, testimony fails: the sound of one hand clapping" (68). As I read these lines, this illuminating comment means that, "For rights claims to be recognized, activists turned life narrators need to ensure their texts succeed in affecting their reader before they can effect change" (Martínez García 2019c, 256). Affect and impact are thus interlocked so one cannot be conceived without the other in testimonial life writing.

Bridging the Online/Offline Divide

With the rise of smartphone technology and other digital advances, we live permanently on the move with a connected device at hand and separating what happens online from what happens offline is no longer easy. In the case of life-writing activists, this poses more benefits than problems.[5] While some of us are currently going on mobile-free rest cures, human rights defenders stay alert and update their social media profiles at every opportunity, aiming to reach wider, dispersed audiences. Yet, the rise of social networking sites or SNS affects the very idea of authorship (see Maguire 2018). But the interplay of digital and more traditional ways of writing the self needs to be further addressed.

Not only do young life writers increasingly employ various means of communication at once, but also the self they choose to present in each of these platforms is sometimes at odds with the version they present elsewhere. "Both offline and online," as Smith and Watson put it in "Virtually Me" (2014), "the autobiographical subject can be approached as an ensemble or assemblage of subject positions through which self-understanding and self-positioning are negotiated" (71). Each of these self-presentation acts, or performances of the self, serves to exemplify life writing in the making and "presents activists with new powerful weapons" (Martínez García 2018, 488). The Internet has, moreover, blurred the limits of private and public self (McNeill and Zuern 2015, xii). Such blurring is, far from negative, an intrinsic feature of our times. Public and private, as much as online and offline, are so interrelated and part of our lives as to be inseparable.[6] Young women activists' life writing, broadly understood, does this in imaginative ways (Martínez García 2018). The book will showcase, in each of the following chapters, other examples where the interplay of online and offline realms makes for a far more impactful kind of activism. What is especially relevant and novel about my study is the variety of multiplatform self-narration modes deployed by young women from the Global South that constitute a central part of contemporary life. Their ubiquitous nature (see Martínez García 2020), online and offline, helps disseminate their agenda at ever faster speeds, and, at the same time, construct a self that is always on the move.

Strategic Narrative Empathy

As a brief summary of the highly contentious notion of empathy, philosopher Martha C. Nussbaum (2012) defines it as the ability "to see the world from another's viewpoint" (36), which bears a close relationship to theories of reader reception: "We integrate what we have read into our reading of other texts and into our way of looking at ourselves and the world" (Schwarz 2001, 15). Cognitivists have pointed to a link between literature and "pro-social behavior" (Hammond and Kim 2014, 7–8). The idea that empathy is related to "prosocial" behavior had earlier been proposed by social psychologists such as Nancy Eisenberg (1982). The "empathy-altruism hypothesis" posed by C. Daniel Batson (1991) has, however, been subject to criticism. Thus, Amy Shuman (2005) argues that an empathic stance may create voyeurs out of readers (5). The answer may well lie in distinguishing empathy from identification, as Dominick LaCapra (2001) suggests: "empathy may be contrasted with identification (as fusion with the other) insofar as empathy marks the point at which the other is indeed recognized and respected as other, and one does not feel compelled or authorized to speak in the other's voice or to take the other's place, for example, as surrogate victim or perpetrator" (27). Through the lens of empathy, therefore, life narratives that deal with human rights abuse lead the public to understand why injustice is unacceptable and consider their role in making changes.

Suzanne Keen's theory of narrative empathy has so far been applied to life writing in few exceptional cases (Anderst 2015; Davis 2016; Baena 2016; Keen 2016; Martínez García 2017a, 2019b, c). This book will be the first book-length attempt to propose the concept of "strategic narrative empathy" (Keen 2008) as a useful tool, in combination with a life-writing theoretical framework, to look at the narrative construction of human rights life-writing projects.

Keen (2016) sees authorial "strategic narrative empathy" as "representational techniques aimed at moving their readers ... especially the case of nonfiction narratives that link up with the advancement of human rights" (20). Among the three types of authorial narrative empathy discussed by

Keen, two stand out in most young women activists' life writing: "ambassadorial strategic empathy" (20) and "broadcast strategic empathy" (22). When "ambassadorial strategic empathy" is deployed to bring to light a current cause by focusing on a group of individuals to whom the reader does not belong and whose life is at stake, as Keen cautions, such time-sensitive causes have sell-by dates (20). On the other hand, "broadcast strategic empathy" employs "universals that will reach everyone" thus overcoming the durability criteria of "less robust forms of strategic empathizing" (22). Keen concludes that texts may blend "empathetic appeals" to secure durability (22). With this in mind, I argue that the life writers discussed in this book make use of both ambassadorial and broadcast empathy to a point where their message will persist the passing of time. As Keen defines it, "strategic empathizing works by calling upon familiarity; it attempts to transcend differences in order to deflect biased reactions to characters from out-groups. It can also rely on representations of universal human experience to connect through shared feelings" (20). I focus on precisely how these are enacted, as I explore the "narrative devices" that draw the reader in by calling on "common human experiences, feelings, hopes, and vulnerabilities" (22), namely the choice of pronouns, emphatic repetition, rhetorical questions, humor, and the appeal to common human experiences and feelings that binds them all. Indeed, these practices are all intertwined, and progressively combined in later texts, as young girl activists become adult women. In what follows, I look at how the texts by these young women illustrate what human rights life-writing projects can do. Specifically, I signal the way these texts deploy empathy as a call to action. In order to do that, I track what Martínez García calls "empathetic mechanisms" (2016), resorting to universal topics that promote the articulation of an emotional bond in such a way as to "move people in two distinct ways – emotionally and to action" (127). These mechanisms are designed to lead people to share the life writer's feelings and want to help her in her fight for social justice. Thus, she—each of the young women activists detailed below—appeals to our shared experience of childhood, adolescence, human emotions, and the multiple channels through which she may connect with an international readership and mobilize empathy.

Six Young Women Activists

This book takes a closer look at the whole life-writing projects of six current key icons of human rights activism and advocacy: Malala Yousafzai, Hyeonseo Lee, Yeonmi Park, Bana Alabed, Nujeen Mustafa, and Nadia Murad. What brings these six case studies together is their coming from the Global South (broadly understood, spanning countries as varied as North Korea, Pakistan, Syria, and Iraq, affected by a diverse range of sociopolitical and economic issues), their gender and age (they were young girls when they witnessed and/or experienced human rights violations), their global advocacy (starting from a very concise social justice issue, they broaden their scope to include other people's fights), their strategic use of English as a rights lingua franca, their deployment of online/offline methods, and resorting to empathy to generate acute social awareness (Martínez García 2016, 2017a, b, 2018). Building on my previous work, each chapter looks at the intriguing ways these activists write themselves, thereby righting the wrongs committed against them, reframing their story as that of an empowered survivor who "[e]xtricat[es] herself from a vulnerable position of victimhood" (2019a, 206).

Notes

1. Multiple life-writing scholars have engaged with the impact of technological advances. See Smith and Watson (2010), McNeill (2014), McNeill and Zuern (2015), Cardell (2014), Cardell et al. (2017), Douglas (2017b), Martínez García (2018), and Morrison (2019).
2. Life writing and media scholars alike have turned to the issue of mediation from multiple angles to explore their interconnectedness (see Poletti and Rak 2014; Poletti 2017; Coletu 2017). I take a different approach to mediation here, however, as I see the digital paradigm opening up spaces for self-expression which for some subjects, particularly the underprivileged and disenfranchised, were previously impossible to access. In that sense, then, fewer layers of mediation are needed for young women activists from the Global South to enter the public sphere.
3. Kate Douglas's (2017a) study of Malala Yousafzai's "collaborative archive" is a forerunning example of how to analyze all life-writing texts, both online and offline, as part of a life narrative. Similarly, Martínez García's (2019a) study of Yousafzai's life-writing texts on and offline guides the approach for this book, where it is expanded to account for novel methods of self-representation for young women life writers.
4. See also Martínez García (2017b, 2018, 2019b, c).

5. Studies of cyberactivism (McCaughey and Ayers 2003) or digital activism (Joyce 2010) tend to claim the positive effects this has had on producing actual social change, e.g., the Arab Spring in the Middle East, the Indignados in Spain, etc. However, most scholars now accept the limitations of doing activism solely online (see Gerbaudo 2012). Taking a cue from Gerbaudo's work and thus a middle-ground approach between cyberoptimism (Shirky 2011) and cyberpessimism (Morozov 2011), this book reflects on how twenty-first-century youth activism relies on a combination of both the old and the new paradigms for narrating themselves and their struggles.
6. The "relative newness" (McNeill and Zuern 2019, 133) of this living at once on and offline makes it hard to discern whether the characteristics displayed in the chosen case studies will in some years become either obsolete or, perhaps, commonplace in life-writing projects—another regular feature of the contemporary "networked self" (Papacharissi 2011, 307).

Works Cited

Anderst, Leah. 2015. Feeling with Real Others: Narrative Empathy in the Autobiographies of Doris Lessing and Alison Bechdel. *Narrative* 23 (3): 271–290.

Baena, Rosalía. 2016. No Pity: Disability Memoirs and Narrative Empathy in Robert Murphy's *The Body Silent* and Reynolds Price's *A Whole New Life*. *Concentric: Literary and Cultural Studies* 42 (2): 65–83.

Batson, C. Daniel. 1991. *The Altruism Question: Toward a Social-Psychological Answer*. Hillsdale, NJ: Lawrence Erlbaum.

Beverley, John. 1987. Anatomía del testimonio. *Revista de Crítica Literaria Latinoamericana* 25: 7–16.

Butler, Judith. 2004. *Precarious Life: The Powers of Mourning and Violence*. London: Verso.

———. 2005. *Giving an Account of Oneself*. New York: Fordham University Press.

———. 2009. *Frames of War: When Is Life Grievable?* London: Verso.

Cardell, Kylie. 2014. *Dear World: Contemporary Uses of the Diary*. Madison: University of Wisconsin Press.

Cardell, Kylie, Kate Douglas, and Emma Maguire. 2017. "Stories": Social Media and Ephemeral Narratives as Memoir. In *Mediating Memory: Tracing the Limits of Memoir*, ed. Bunty Avieson, Fiona Giles, and Sue Joseph, 157–172. New York: Routledge.

Coletu, Ebony. 2017. Biographic Mediation. *a/b: Auto/Biography Studies* 32 (2): 384–385.

Couser, G. Thomas. 2004. *Vulnerable Subjects: Ethics and Life Writing*. Ithaca, NY: Cornell University Press.
Davis, Rocio. 2016. Empathy and Life Writing. *Concentric: Literary and Cultural Studies* 42 (2): 3–8.
Douglas, Kate. 2010. *Contesting Childhood: Autobiography, Trauma and Memory*. New Brunswick, NY: Rutgers University Press.
———. 2015. Ethical Dialogues: Youth, Memoir and Trauma. *a/b: Auto/Biography Studies* 30 (2): 271–288.
———. 2017a. Malala Yousafzai, Life Narrative and the Collaborative Archive. *Life Writing* 14 (3): 297–311.
———. 2017b. Youth, Trauma and Memorialisation: The Selfie as Witnessing. *Memory Studies*: 1–16.
Douglas, Kate, and Anna Poletti. 2016. *Life Narratives and Youth Culture: Representation, Agency and Participation*. London: Palgrave Macmillan.
Douglas, Kate, and Kylie Cardell. 2015. *Telling Tales: Autobiographies of Childhood and Youth*. Abingdon: Routledge.
Eakin, Paul John (ed.). 2004. *The Ethics of Life Writing*. Ithaca, NY: Cornell University Press.
Eisenberg, Nancy (ed.). 1982. *The Development of Prosocial Behavior*. New York: Academic Press.
Gerbaudo, Paolo. 2012. *Tweets and the Streets: Social Media and Contemporary Activism*. London: Pluto Press.
Gilmore, Leigh. 2001. *The Limits of Autobiography: Trauma and Testimony*. Ithaca: Cornell University Press.
———. 2017a. *Tainted Witness: Why We Doubt What Women Say About Their Lives*. New York: Columbia University Press.
———. 2017b. Testimony. *a/b: Auto/Biography Studies* 32 (2): 307–309.
Gilmore, Leigh, and Elizabeth Marshall. 2019. *Witnessing Girlhood: Toward an Intersectional Tradition of Life Writing*. New York: Fordham University Press.
Hammond, Meghan Marie, and Sue J. Kim. 2014. *Rethinking Empathy Through Literature*. New York: Routledge.
Hesford, Wendy S. 2011. *Spectacular Rhetorics: Human Rights Visions, Recognitions, Feminisms*. Durham, NC: Duke University Press.
Joyce, Mary (ed.). 2010. *Digital Activism Decoded: The New Mechanics of Change*. New York: International Debate Education Association.
Kearney, Richard. 1996. Narrative and Ethics. *Proceedings of the Aristotelian Society* 70: 29–45.
Keen, Suzanne. 2008. Strategic Empathizing: Techniques of Bounded, Ambassadorial, and Broadcast Narrative Empathy. *Deutsche Vierteljahrsschrift für Literaturwissenchaft und Geistesgeschichte* 82 (3): 477–493.
———. 2016. Life Writing and the Empathetic Circle. *Concentric: Literary and Cultural Studies* 42 (2): 9–26.

LaCapra, Dominick. 2001. *Writing History, Writing Trauma*. Baltimore: Johns Hopkins University Press.

Maguire, Emma. 2018. *Girls, Autobiography, Media Gender and Self-Mediation in Digital Economies*. Palgrave Macmillan.

Martínez García, Ana Belén. 2016. Narrative Emotions and Human Rights Life Writing. In *On the Move: Glancing Backwards to Build a Future in English Studies*, ed. Aitor Ibarrola-Armendariz and Jon Ortiz de Urbina Arruabarrena, 127–132. Bilbao: University of Deusto.

———. 2017a. Unearthing the Past: Bringing Ideological Indoctrination to Light in North Korean Girls' Memoirs. *a/b: Auto/Biography Studies* 32 (3): 587–602.

———. 2017b. Bana Alabed: Using Twitter to Draw Attention to Human Rights Violations. *Prose Studies: History, Theory, Criticism* 39 (2–3): 132–149.

———. 2018. TED Talks as Life Writing: Online and Offline Activism. *Life Writing* 15 (4): 487–503.

———. 2019a. Construction and Collaboration in Life-Writing Projects: Malala Yousafzai's Activist 'I'. *Journal of Writing in Creative Practice* 12 (1–2): 201–217.

———. 2019b. Denouncing Human Trafficking in China: North Korean Women's Memoirs as Evidence. *State Crime Journal* 8 (1): 59–79.

———. 2019c. Empathy for Social Justice: The Case of Malala Yousafzai. *Journal of English Studies* 17: 253–275.

———. 2020. Women Activists' Strategies of Online Self-Presentation. *AI & Society: Journal of Knowledge, Culture and Communication*: Special Issue on Iteration as Persuasion in a Digital World. Forthcoming.

McCaughey, Martha, and Michael D. Ayers (eds.). 2003. *Cyberactivism: Online Activism in Theory and Practice*. New York: Routledge.

McNeill, Laurie. 2014. Life Bytes: Six-Word Memoir and the Exigencies of Auto/Tweetographies. In *Identity Technologies: Constructing the Self Online*, ed. Anna Poletti and Julie Rak, 144–164. Madison: University of Wisconsin Press.

McNeill, Laurie, and John David Zuern. 2015. Online Lives 2.0: Introduction. *Biography* 38 (2): v–xlvi.

———. 2019. Reading Digital Lives Generously. In *Research Methodologies for Auto/Biography Studies*, ed. Kate Douglas and Ashley Barnwell, 132–139. New York: Routledge.

Menchú, Rigoberta. 1984. *I, Rigoberta Menchú: An Indian Woman in Guatemala*, ed. Elisabeth Burgos-Debray and trans. Ann Wright. London: Verso.

———. 2020. Rigoberta Menchú Tum (@RigobertMenchu). *Twitter*. Accessed 11 February 2020.

Morrison, Aimée. 2019. Social, Media, Life Writing: Online Lives at Scale, Up Close, and In Context. In *Research Methodologies for Auto/Biography Studies*, ed. Kate Douglas and Ashley Barnwell, 41–48. New York: Routledge.
Morozov, Evgeny. 2011. *The Net Delusion: How Not to Liberate the World*. London: Penguin.
Nussbaum, Martha C. 2001. *Upheavals of Thought: The Intelligence of Emotions*. Cambridge: Cambridge University Press.
———. 2012. *Not for Profit: Why Democracy Needs the Humanities*. Princeton: Princeton University Press.
Papacharissi, Zizi (ed.). 2011. *A Networked Self: Identity, Community, and Culture on Social Network Sites*. New York: Routledge.
Poletti, Anna. 2017. What's Next? Mediation. *a/b: Auto/Biography Studies* 32 (2): 263–266.
Poletti, Anna, and Julie Rak (eds.). 2014. *Identity Technologies: Constructing the Self Online*. Madison: University of Wisconsin Press.
Schaffer, Kay, and Sidonie Smith. 2004. *Human Rights and Narrated Lives: The Ethics of Recognition*. New York: Palgrave Macmillan.
Schwarz, Daniel R. 2001. A Humanistic Ethics of Reading. In *Mapping the Ethical Turn: A Reader in Ethics, Culture, and Literary Theory*, ed. T.F. Davis and K. Womack, 3–15. Charlottesville: University Press of Virginia.
Shirky, Clay. 2011. The Political Power of Social Media: Technology, the Public Sphere, and Political Change. *Foreign Affairs* 90 (1): 28–41.
Shuman, Amy. 2005. *Other People's Stories: Entitlement Claims and the Critique of Empathy*. Urbana: University of Illinois Press.
Smith, Sidonie. 2006. Narratives and Rights: *Zlata's Diary* and the Circulation of Stories of Suffering Ethnicity. *WSQ: Women's Studies Quarterly* 34 (1&2): 133–152.
Smith, Sidonie, and Julia Watson (eds.). 1992. *De/Colonizing the Subject: The Politics of Gender in Women's Autobiography*. Minneapolis: University of Minnesota Press.
———. 1996. *Getting a Life: Everyday Uses of Autobiography*. Minneapolis: University of Minnesota Press.
———. 1998. *Women, Autobiography, Theory: A Reader*. Madison: University of Wisconsin Press.
———. 2002. *Interfaces: Women, Autobiography, Image, Performance*. Minneapolis: University of Minnesota Press.
Smith, Sidonie, and Julia Watson. 2010. *Reading Autobiography: A Guide for Interpreting Life Narratives*, 2nd ed. Minneapolis: Minnesota University Press.
———. 2012. Witness or False Witness?: Metrics of Authenticity, Collective I-Formations, and the Ethic of Verification in First-Person Testimony. *Biography* 35 (4): 590–626.

———. 2014. Virtually Me: A Toolbox about Online Self-Presentation. In *Identity Technologies: Constructing the Self Online*, ed. Anna Poletti and Julie Rak, 70–95. Madison: University of Wisconsin Press.

———. 2017. *Life Writing in the Long Run: A Smith & Watson Autobiography Studies Reader*. Ann Arbor, MI: Maize Books.

Stoll, David. 1999. *Rigoberta Menchú and the Story of All Poor Guatemalans*. Boulder: Westview.

———. David Stoll Breaks the Silence. 2001. In *The Rigoberta Menchú Controversy*, ed. Arturo Arias, 118–120. Minneapolis: University of Minnesota Press.

Whitlock, Gillian. 2007. *Soft Weapons: Autobiography in Transit*. Chicago: University of Chicago Press.

———. 2015. *Postcolonial Life Narratives: Testimonial Transactions*. Oxford: Oxford University Press.

CHAPTER 2

Malala Yousafzai: Fighting for Girls' Rights via Collaboration and Co-construction

Abstract Building on academic publications that have tried to assess Malala Yousafzai's life-writing project in its entirety, this chapter presents each of her life-writing texts as an example of collaborative testimonial narrative. Moving away from an objective, neutral tone, her life writing tends to rely on emotional language and various other discursive strategies aimed at sustaining interest over time. Since Malala Yousafzai started her self-narration when she was 11, technology and traditional media have gone hand in hand. Her appropriation of the hashtag launched under her name proved vital in her reconstruction of an activist self. Yet, the presence of a co-author, either hinted at or made explicit, can be traced throughout all her life-writing texts, from her first blog to her last book on displacement.

This chapter builds on an original article first published as "Construction and Collaboration in Life-Writing Projects: Malala Yousafzai's Activist 'I'" (Martínez García 2019a) in the *Journal of Writing in Creative Practice* 12 (1–2): 201–217. It also features part of an original article first published as "Empathy for Social Justice: The Case of Malala Yousafzai" (Martínez García 2019c) in the *Journal of English Studies* 17: 253–275.

A. B. Martínez García, *New Forms of Self-Narration*, Palgrave Studies in Life Writing, https://doi.org/10.1007/978-3-030-46420-2_2

Keywords Malala Yousafzai · Co-construction · Life-writing project · Collaborative testimonial narrative · Emotional language · Discursive strategies

Born in Pakistan in 1997, Malala Yousafzai has become a public figure worldwide who is known only by her first name and whose name stands for the right for girls' education. This is primarily so because of the Taliban's attempt to silence her activism by shooting her at close range. She has led a public life from girlhood, beginning with ablog she wrote for the BBC when she was eleven (Anon. 2009). Then, she appeared in two *New York Times* documentaries (Ellick 2009; Ellick and Ashraf 2009), between the ages of eleven and twelve, which might have revealed her identity and cause the terrorist attack that made her a global icon. That happened in October 2012 when she was fifteen. Since her recovery after the near-fatal shot, once relocated in England, she has become an advocate for the cause of girls' education worldwide, going on to speak at the United Nations (2013, 2015, 2017) and to win the Nobel Peace Prize (Malala Fund 2014). Soon becoming a celebrity, receiving international support and peace awards, she has actively pursued activism as a form of self-construction. Before adulthood, she published a celebrated co-authored autobiography with Christina Lamb (Yousafzai and Lamb 2013), founded several charitable works worldwide (Malala Fund 2017a), and released a documentary film titled *He Named Me Malala* (Guggenheim 2015). In 2017, no longer a child, she was interviewed on her role as an adult in fighting for girls' rights (Gidda 2017) and gained prominence after a period of silence by her open letter to United States President Donald Trump (Malala Fund 2017b, c) and her Girl Power Trip (Malala Fund 2017d). In April 2017, she became the youngest-ever UN Messenger of Peace (Anon. 2017a) then launched her own Twitter account using the easily recognizable first name handle @Malala (Yousafzai 2020a), thus seemingly independent of Malala Fund. These narratives configure a larger life-writing project authored by, at least in part, Malala (Douglas 2017). Exploring the fluctuating rhythms of writing the self offline and online, I will seek to extricate the mechanisms by which Malala makes an efficient call to action still in adulthood.

Constructing an Activist "I"

A feature inextricably linked to Malala's life-writing project is the fact that all her life writing presents a collaborative nature. There is always somebody else involved in the process of writing the story of her life, be that a translator, editor, journalist, activist, manager, or several of these figures. This is a vital issue to take into account, as it poses potential problems to the nature of her autobiographical "voice" (Smith and Watson 2010, 79–85). Some would argue that it detracts from her authenticity; however, life writing may raise questions relating to its "truth" (Smith and Watson 2012). What interests me here is how Malala's voice manages to come across as both authentic and reliable, doing so by wielding a powerful usage of discursive strategies devised to garner empathy and foster understanding and support (Whitlock 2007, 2015; Keen 2016; Martínez García 2016; Smith and Watson 2017; Simonsen and Kjaergård 2017). One is faced with the problematics surrounding complex notions of the self, a self not only constructed on and offline, but also co-constructed. In her essay on "Testimony," Leigh Gilmore (2017) highlights the value of such autobiographical "co-construction":

> A focus on testimony–those verbal acts in which a person bears witness to harm in a public forum–enables us to see how histories of harm and first-person witness intertwine and why their co-construction is so crucial to parsing life narrative. (307)

Malala's co-constructed life narrative started with the blog she wrote for the BBC (Anon. 2009).[1] As she would later admit, she did not write it as it is presented online (Anon. 2009). The process of writing was a complex, multimodal one, involving pen and pencil, as well as a computer, a phone, and a witness/journalist/translator (Yousafzai and Lamb 2013, 129–130). However, one must attend to the ethical urgency in the blog entries, to the empathic call that they make and to the way an activist self is constructed or co-constructed. Thus, for example, the title of her first entry was "I am afraid" (Anon. 2009), the reason being that girls had been banned from school and she felt her life was at risk on the street, which speaks for the situation of the collective of Swati girls, subject to the Taliban dictates in the area at the time. In so doing, as Sidonie Smith and Julia Watson note, the narrating "I" affirms the "*duty to narrate a collective story*" (2012, 594; original emphasis).

Almost by accident, Malala featured in a documentary on education in Pakistan. She was not the intended interviewee, but she caught the eye of one of the directors who was struck by her innocent looks, beauty, and heartfelt emotion when asked about the prospects of getting an education in her country (Ellick and Ashraf 2009; Ellick 2009). In her memoir, she remembers one of her most famous lines: "I told the documentary makers, 'They cannot stop *me*. *I* will get *my* education if it's at home, school or somewhere else. This is *our* request to the world – to save *our* schools, save *our* Pakistan, save *our* Swat'" (Yousafzai and Lamb 2013, 135; emphasis added). The shifting perspective, from the first-person singular to the first-person plural, together with the emphatic repetition of short phrases are strategies that, as proved here, remind readers of her texts that her discourse was originally as complex as it is now when she started speaking out against the ban on girls' education at the age of 11.

Due to Malala's outspokenness in Pakistani media as well as her not so hidden anonymous identity as the girl behind the blog, the Taliban targeted her and her family. All the while thinking that they would attempt to kill her father first, she continued to go to school when allowed to do so (not every day, due to the ban she had mentioned in her texts). Thus, one day, on her way to school, she was shot, prompting a flood of news coverage of unprecedented dimensions. Skipping the media campaign, I focus on the iconicity she gained thereafter. While she was in Birmingham hospital, former United Kingdom's Prime Minister and UN Special Envoy for Global Education Gordon Brown launched a campaign to petition the Pakistani government to implement policies on girls' education (Melancon 2012). The petition was set up as a website in Malala's name (www.iammalala.org), now discontinued, calling on Pakistan and the world to educate all children, including girls (Brown 2012). Rights activists urged people to sign the petition and join the conversation on Twitter with the hashtag #IamMalala. In fact, in the first two weeks, approximately one million people signed the petition (Brown 2012). Upon recovery, Malala made the hashtag #IamMalala her own motto, thus adopting a radical stance and a renewed, if not new, self. She tries to come across as what people in the Global North see in her, a girl shot because she wanted to go to school. The injustice of the attack is then maximized to epic proportions. But, at the same time, by reclaiming the hashtag, she starts reconstructing her identity on and offline, she emerges as an empowered individual that no longer requires someone to speak for her: Her "I" is a powerful agent, drawing from traditions of human rights, testimonial writing, and ethics, using available templates at her disposal to generate empathic concern and support for her cause (Smith and Watson 2010, 134).

Malala's speech before the United Nations on 12 July 2013 and other interviews must be read alongside the life stories that have shaped who she is. She acknowledges, for example, the legacy of Martin Luther King, Gandhi, Mother Teresa, and her role model, Benazir Bhutto (United Nations 2013). As for discursive strategies, the rhetorical emphatic repetition of certain phrases is noteworthy. Thus, Malala calls upon "dear brothers and sisters" eight times, aiming to establish an emotional connection with the audience that moves beyond geopolitical borders, a connection that bypasses issues of ethnicity, religion, culture, or social class and appeals to the common bond of the human family. It is a strategy embedded in human rights discourse, as Sidonie Smith (2006) notes in "Narratives and Rights," which "contributes to a paradox at the heart of human rights discourse and practice: the uneasy enfolding of the universal in the ethnic particular" (134). Activism is of pivotal importance in shaping the identity Malala is creating. She therefore emphasizes the verb "speak" repeating it eight times as well (United Nations 2013). "Child" appears fourteen times, while "women" appears eleven times and "girl" a mere six times. However, the word "right" is the most prominent of all her words, featuring sixteen times. She makes a point of insisting on the different but connected rights that are at stake when discussing education—children's rights, women's rights, and human rights encompassing them all. "Education" and related words such as "educational" make nineteen appearances, clearly the topic by which she aims to define herself. By looking closely at the words that she uses the most, one gets a sense of the education activist self she is in the process of constructing.

Global mass media and online communication platforms had an important role in Malala's jump to stardom in the ensuing months. YouTube, I argue, was a helpful distributor of her message. Her UN speech has now more than 2.5 million views (United Nations 2013). On International Women's Day 2017, the BBC broadcasted a concert featuring Malala's speech put to music and recited by many different voices (Media Centre 2017). Composer Kate Whitley explains she was inspired by this speech because the key to Malala's language is that it is very simple, but precisely because it is that simple, she uses it to make very powerful statements (Radio 3 2017). As one of the performers further points out, the speech "homes in on one of the greatest injustices ... without education, we are all condemned to repeat the mistakes of the past" (Radio 3 2017). In this especially commissioned piece, repetition is also strikingly insistent upon the potential for global education for all: "let us pick up our books and pens" is the center of the chorus's interventions (Whitley 2017). Some of the speech's most memorable phrases have similarly become embedded in other campaigns, notably for girls' rights, women's rights, or education activism in general. Malala's message may have resurfaced in bigger or smaller fights thanks to her repetitive—though at times nuanced—style. Thinking back at the terms she most repeated throughout her UN speech (United Nations 2013), those phrases become apparent in current ongoing campaigns off and online.

Appropriating the Hashtag, Rewriting Her Identity

Malala's memoir, *I Am Malala: The Girl Who Stood Up for Education and Was Shot by the Taliban*, was first published on 8 October 2013 (Yousafzai and Lamb 2013). The book soon became a bestseller, entering prominent lists like the *New York Times*, where it featured among nonfiction best sellers for 52 weeks ranking #5 among nonfiction books in June 2016 (Anon. 2016), and Amazon, where it ranked in its audible format, as of 11 July 2017, #1 among memoirs (Anon. 2017b) and #4 among women's biographies (Anon. 2017c). It has sold over 1.8 million copies (Chabba 2016), been translated to 40 languages (Sutton 2017), and edited for young readers. This latter edition, entitled *I Am Malala: How One Girl Stood Up for Education and Changed the World* (Yousafzai and McCormick 2014), was published in 2014 and ranked, as of 11 July 2017, #1 among teen and young adult social activist biographies on Amazon (Anon. 2017d). Along with marketing success, it has been included in curricular and extracurricular activities across the globe, with teachers and pupils of various educational levels contributing to Malala's iconicity—a girl fighting for girls' universal right to education (Malala Fund 2017a).

Apart from Malala's appropriation of the hashtag earlier mentioned, which features in the memoir's title, she asserts her identity throughout the book, but most notably at two key points—in the last lines of both her prologue and her epilogue. Thus, the sentence is placed at three strategic places—title, beginning, and end. If the prologue is an assertion that this memoir will tell readers details by Malala herself, the way it is phrased illustrates an authenticity claim: "Who is Malala? *I am Malala* and this is my story" (Yousafzai and Lamb 2013, 6; emphasis added). At the end, she assures readers she is still the same Malala, something she has often said in interviews, insisting she remains unchanged even after gaining international fame: "*I am Malala*. My world has changed but I have not" (Yousafzai and Lamb 2013, 265; emphasis added). Yet, only one chapter before this epilogue, she closes by doubting whether to identify with the image others have of her: "When people talk about the way I was shot and what happened I think it's the story of Malala, 'a girl shot by the Taliban'; I don't feel it's a story about me at all" (Yousafzai and Lamb 2013, 255). Few readers have focused on this peculiar comment that I see central toward understanding the layered complexity of Malala Yousafzai's life-writing process. On the one hand, she wishes to continue her activism, so the fact that she is a celebrity may indeed help, promoting visibility and advocacy. On the other hand, it is difficult to say whether she has been subsumed into the identity others have created for her. By assuming the hashtag, one she had not created, she becomes that Malala, the Malala that equals a girl shot by the Taliban. Nevertheless, thanks to her being known as that girl, she is in a position of relative power to face those who attempted to silence her. Extricating herself from a vulnerable position of victimhood, she finds strength in raising her voice, claiming her name for herself, and encouraging others to raise their voices too. Rather than letting others speak for her, she is the one speaking for herself and for other children whose education is threatened. She becomes an empowered individual, challenging the fear that made her not respond to the attackers that fateful day when they stopped the bus and asked the girls inside who was Malala. "I am Malala," caught in her throat, was left unsaid. Now, Malala's narrative is her "survivor narrative" (Alcoff and Gray-Rosendale 1996, 220). Even if silent at that time, now she is both speaking up and speaking out, raising her voice and raising awareness. Overcoming fear and telling her story, she finds courage: "Who is Malala? I am Malala and this is my story" (Yousafzai and Lamb 2013, 6). That movement from inaction to action makes her more relatable. Quite tellingly, she uses both a rhetorical question and a simple repetitive structure to emphasize her transformation into an activist.

Malala resorts to visual aids to enhance empathy and draw the reader into her experience. Numerous photographs include Malala as a child, from the time she was a baby until she started giving speeches at school (52i–viii). A further set of photographs focuses on the shooting, depicting events that happened shortly before and afterward (212i–viii). Visual identification is a vehicle of empathy as it heightens connections and supports referentiality. Malala Yousafzai's strategy is similar to Zlata

Filipović's in highlighting the image of an innocent child as a means to generating humanitarian affects. As Smith notes when discussing *Zlata's Diary* and its use of photographs, "The innocence effect is … reinforced through the packaging … and the paratextual use of photographs that visualize the young girl's story as a sentimentalized drama of lost childhood" (2006, 144). Apart from providing a sympathetic reading, the photographs transform the reader into a witness. Among the various photographs, we find some of the notes that she, with trembling hand, wrote when recovering from her head wound in hospital: "When will my father come? We dont [sic] have alot [sic] of money? - Now my hair is small [sic] … Hwo [sic] did this to me? Stop fights [sic] What happend [sic] to me?" (Yousafzai and Lamb 2013, 236–237). The quivering handwriting, emphasized by the spelling mistakes, *shakes* the reader's consciousness. It is as if one could see the shaky hand that wrote those things. The narrating "I" calls for a compassionate "humanitarian reading" (Slaughter 2009), involving the reader, who feels the ethical responsibility to denounce the situation that allows children to be targeted just because they want an education.

Malala's "I" coexists throughout her memoir with a collective pronoun "we" that varies in meaning depending on the group she identifies with. Smith and Watson (2012) argue that testimonies tend to rely on a narrating "I" that encompasses collective plights (600). However, Malala's texts offer an example of how the "I" and the "we" fluctuate and stand in dynamic tension. From the start, Malala makes a strong point of identifying with the Pashtun, an ethnic and cultural subgroup of her region, Swat valley, geographically spanning parts of Pakistan and Afghanistan. In fact, this identity opens the first chapter: "When I was born, people in our village commiserated with my mother and nobody congratulated my father. I arrived at dawn as the last star blinked out. *We Pashtuns* see this as an auspicious sign" (Yousafzai and Lamb 2013, 9; emphasis added). Though Pashtuns think a woman's place is "to prepare food and give birth to children" (9), her father defied tradition by celebrating, writing her name on the family tree—which is traditionally reserved for male offspring—and choosing a heroine's name—Malalai of Maiwand, who defied societal rules stipulating the place of a woman was inside the home by going on a battlefield to inspire the Afghan troops fighting the British. Malala's name, inspired by this Pashtun folk heroine, is from the beginning something others have thought of for her, even if for very good reasons. Malala's life writing, then, may be regarded as an exploration of the self, a way of writing her own version of herself, forging an identity that fits not only whatever molds others have in mind but her very own. A noticeable shift from the first-person plural to the singular takes place while talking about her grandmother's village traditions. Then, she moves from the "we" to the "I" in order to distance herself from what she considers not so laudable traditions. She deploys the "I" to make a strong statement: "I am very proud to be a Pashtun but sometimes I think our code of conduct has a lot to answer for, particularly where the treatment of women is concerned" (54). Further, she relates how she has been told of girls forced and sold into marriage or even killed because of defying parental wishes.

The narrative draws a line between "us" and the rest of the world when the "we" is meant to stand for "Pakistani schoolgirls." One of the most emotional examples of deploying the first-person plural takes place when Malala describes how they acted and felt after a partial ban lift on girls' education:

> The pressure from the whole country worked, and Fazlullah agreed to lift the ban for girls up to ten years old – Year 4. I was in Year 5 and *some of us* pretended *we* were younger than *we* were. *We* started going to school again, dressed in ordinary clothes and hiding *our* books under *our* shawls. It was risky but it was the only ambition I had back then ...
>
> Some people are afraid of ghosts, some of spiders or snakes – in those days *we* were afraid of *our* fellow human beings. (138–139; emphasis added)

Now a human rights activist, it is remarkable that Malala doubted her "fellow human beings" at that point. It is especially heart-wrenching, since her current activist discourse as a Nobel Peace Prize recipient and United Nations Ambassador of Peace hinges on her insistence that "Islam is a religion of peace" (United Nations 2013), provided it is not appropriated as ideology by extremists.

A further discursive strategy is Malala's rewriting of tradition, an effort to create an activist self that is still part of Pashtun tradition but innovates it so as to make it fit a feminist template. Throughout her memoir, Malala quotes several Pashto *tapey* or popular folk couplets. She usually leaves them untouched, but for two relevant occasions. Once, when she describes how her grandmother's *tapa* does not fit the times anymore:

> I remembered the *tapa* my grandmother used to recite: 'No Pashtun leaves his land of his own sweet will./ Either he leaves from poverty or he leaves for love.' Now we were being driven out for a third reason the *tapa* writer had never imagined – the Taliban.
> (Yousafzai and Lamb 2013, 147)

Malala takes her implicit criticism further on waking up from the coma at the hospital, when she actually rewrites another *tapa*, thus breaking the norm:

> 'Actually there's a *tapa* I want to rewrite.'
> My father looked intrigued. *Tapey* are the centuries-old collected wisdom of our society; you don't change them. 'Which one?' he asked.
> 'This one,' I said.
>
> If the men cannot win the battle, O my country,
> Then the women will come forth and win you an honour.
> ...
>
> I wanted to change it to:
>
> Whether the men are winning or losing the battle, O my country,
> The women are coming and the women will win you an honour.
> (249–250)

This reworking of tradition fits in with Malala's feminist agenda of wishing to give women a voice. By rewriting *tapey*, she is both true to her cultural identity and innovatively seeking to bring it closer to women's subjectivity and empowerment. By her rewriting act, she brings together oral tradition and oral history, making herself and a woman's voice part of that tradition. The move is strategic and reverberates in her current activism for women's rights.

Media and Mediation

On 10 December 2014, Malala Yousafzai became the youngest recipient of the Nobel Peace Prize. In her acceptance speech before the Nobel Committee in Oslo, she stressed the importance of actions over words. Thinking about children that are kept out of school, she said: "it is not time to pity them; it is time to take action" (Malala Fund 2014). On strategic empathizing grounds (Keen 2016), she resorts to the rhetoric of discursive parallel opposition: "it is not time to ... it is time to ..." (Malala Fund 2014). Therefore, even though she has referred to compassion as a basic human need, it is in fact necessary to move beyond. Rather, what we need is an empathic approach, one that overcomes pity "to bring about fundamental social change" (Krznaric 2014, ix). Malala chooses to address the terrorists, blaming them for misusing Islam: "Have you not learnt that in the Holy Koran Allah says 'If you kill one person, it is as if you kill the whole humanity'?" (Malala Fund 2014). This rhetorical question, which seeks no answer, comes after several similar sentences, all of them starting the same way: "Have you not learnt ...?" (Malala Fund 2014). Finally, she resorts to standing up for her community, something that she has in common with the tradition of testimony in which her life narrative is inscribed: "I tell my story not because it is unique, but because it is not; it is the story of many girls" (Malala Fund 2014). As we have seen, Malala's eloquent style resorts to frequent repetition for emphasis. In this speech, though Malala is already close to adulthood, she identifies herself as "one child" and claims that children do not understand the so-called war on terror. Thus, she asks: "*Why is it* that countries that we call strong are so powerful in creating wars but are so weak in bringing peace? *Why is it? Why is it* that giving guns is so easy but giving books is so hard? *Why is it? Why is it* that making tanks is so easy but building schools is so hard?" (Malala Fund 2014; emphasis added). Rhetorical repetition adds tension to her speech. The main issue—*Why is it?*—bears no response, thus challenging readers ethically. Resorting to the use of rhetorical questions emotionally loaded and with nuanced repetition is not new; *Zlata's Diary*, commented in depth by Sidonie Smith (2006), is highly reliant on this narrative technique, which is not just how children talk, but one of the rhetorical strategies activists of all ages and backgrounds deploy to great effect in their consciousness-raising discourses. For instance, the strategy is clearly visible in one of the multiple entries where Zlata emotionally calls for the end of the war: "*Will* this war ever *stop? Will* our suffering *stop* ...?" (Filipović 1995, 106; emphasis added). As such, emphatic repetition may be read as one of the empathetic mechanisms suggested in the introduction. These questions "ignite an affective charge" and "serve as a means of shaming" readers (Smith 2006, 148), since the answer to those rhetorical questions is far from simple. Indeed, it seems as if that escapes our control and is in the hands of those in power, but Malala reminds the audience that "we must work, not wait; not just the politicians and world leaders, we all need to contribute – me, you, we; it is our duty" (Malala Fund 2014). Malala's call to action cannot possibly be more straightforward than that. Her choice of pronouns involves readers in her fight: "we ... we all ... me, you, we" (Malala Fund 2014). The fluctuating rhythmic progress of the narrative, shifting from the first-person singular to the first-person plural is strategically devised to involve readers who are called to redress the situation and compelled to do so in moral terms ("it is our duty"). Enjoining the discourse of humanitarianism with moral ethics is a trademark of rights narratives. Gillian Whitlock (2007) notes in *Soft Weapons* how these narratives can elicit an "ethical response" provided "empathic witnessing" takes place (77). Importantly, the collective pronoun combines the force of testimonial accounts of oppressed others with the "ethical witness" position of readers as part of the fight. We are at once distant spectators and operative members of the same community of human beings.

Malala's Nobel Peace Prize speech has almost 6 million views on YouTube (Malala Fund 2014) with images and words becoming part of memes quickly flooding social media platforms at the time and still to date. Some of those edited images or multimedia forms have been ready-made for Malala Fund and UN campaigns, some however have not. The specific technological affordances of Twitter, for instance, have arguably facilitated the virality of her message, even years after the speech was delivered. The platform fosters participation and engagement, for instance by users assuming a hashtag, a still frame, and repurposing it—in other words, what danah boyd (2010) calls "replicability" and "scalability" makes a difference in the potential impact a narrative originally produced offline may have online.[2] The transient nature of the digital matters not when an icon, a motto, can be taken up by other forces. For better or worse (see Ahmed 2014; Rao 2015), just the name Malala still demands recognition. Similarly, just her face is iconic enough for readers/audiences across the globe to identify the person with the cause, namely girls' right to education.

2015 saw the release of *He Named Me Malala* (Guggenheim 2015), a documentary tracking her life in the run-up to the Nobel award ceremony. For lack of space, I will skip in-depth commentary here. The most striking feature, as regards life-writing and discursive strategies, is the fact that though Malala's voice is supposed to come through as evidenced in the title, it does not really feature an empowered "I"—the presence of the director's voice behind the scenes is quite disturbing at times.[3]

As far as social media go, a rapid count reveals the influence Malala instills in the global public sphere and the collaborative nature of her activism. The Malala Fund—founded by Ziauddin and Malala Yousafzai in 2013 to advocate for girls' education—website has broadened its scope to include other voices, with initiatives such as the Gulmakai Network launched in 2017 to honor the pseudonym—Gul Makai—under which she first blogged and to provide support to already existing campaigns led by adults all over the world (Malala Fund 2020a), and Assembly (2020b), a newsletter launched in 2018 that features other girls' voices and life stories. A further mode of approaching the public is via the Malala Fund (2019) YouTube channel, though it only has 71,900 subscribers as of 12 March 2020. For Malala Fund (2020d), Facebook is the most successful platform, boasting 1,021,099 followers, closely followed by Instagram (2020e), which amasses 1,015,221. However, Twitter (2020c) has fewer followers, namely 649,545. Could this be the confluence of fewer images on the latter together with the fact that it is precisely on that SNS where Malala boasts the biggest number of followers? Malala's Facebook account may well have been hacked, with so many people claiming her identity as to be impossible to tell whether she is still using the platform or not. On her personal Instagram (Yousafzai 2020b), though, created in July 2018 for the highly publicized Girl Power Trip she undertook that summer, she is followed by more than a million users—1,263,195 to be precise.

With those high numbers on Instagram and 1,636,382 Twitter followers, Malala Yousafzai (2020a) is admittedly one of the most iconic young women activists of the 2010–2020 decade. In fact, she was chosen for the cover of December 2019 *Teen Vogue* special issue on a "Decade of Youth Rising" which included an interview on the past and present of youth activism, and what the future holds. Thus, she firmly concludes: "the last decade was a decade of youth activism, but the next one is going to be about youth change-making" (Mukhopadhyay 2019).

I Am… We Are

As a coda to this chapter, I turn my attention to the latest of Malala's life-writing texts—her auto/biographical book *We Are Displaced: My Journey and Stories from Refugee Girls around the World* (Yousafzai 2019). From advocating for the right to education in her childhood and teenage years, Malala Yousafzai has evolved into an adult who is also heavily invested in the dire—and urgently current—situation refugees must endure. A notable shift in the strategic use of pronouns can be tracked, from the "I" in the title of her first co-authored memoir (Yousafzai and Lamb 2013), to the "We" in the title of this recent collaborative—though single-authored—publication. In fact, this latest text might be read as a collaborative testimonial narrative (Whitlock 2007, 2015). As has been seen here and elsewhere (Martínez García 2016, 2019a, c), Malala Yousafzai's life-writing project is marked by an awareness that emotional language can garner support for activists, and rhetorical discursive strategies are deployed to that effect. Following Suzanne Keen's (2016) theory of narrative empathy, exploiting the universal but also the particular in the self she presents before readers/audiences, online and offline, crossing from a first-person singular to a first-person plural approach, is geared at exciting a range of emotions at once and the necessary ethical engagement needed for the cause not to subside. One might argue this exemplifies the so often quoted feminist slogan that "the personal is political" in the way an individual story—or many such voices—are raised so that support is garnered, in this case, for the cause of girls' rights, displaced girls' rights to be more specific. Moving away from an objective, neutral tone, "beyond the cold data of statistics" (Martínez García 2019a, 202), Malala Yousafzai's life writing tends to rely on emotional language and various other "narrative empathizing techniques" (Keen 2016) aimed at sustaining interest over time.

In her latest published work, *We Are Displaced* (Yousafzai 2019), Malala harnesses the first-person plural to claim the identity of a displaced person. Even though the experience of being an "IDP" or internally displaced person already featured in *I Am Malala* (Yousafzai and Lamb 2013), since settling in England she has focused her life-writing activism on education as a human right, rather than socioeconomic rights, political rights, or refugee or asylum-seekers' rights. Now the tide has turned. Amid the global crisis in migration, she redefines herself as, not just a young woman fighting for girls' rights, but one who, as a girl, experienced forced migration and so can give voice to others in similar situations. The narrating "I" makes sure to emphasize the difference between being a displaced person or a refugee. They do share similar traits, mostly to do with the inadequate treatment they receive, and the major misunderstandings and fake news created around them. But Malala makes sure not to describe herself as a refugee, something that sets her apart from the rest of the activist life writers the present volume will talk about. As will be seen in subsequent chapters, other young women activists claim or have claimed refugee status in the countries where they have relocated. Though uncomfortable with the ethical baggage of such a word, like Nujeen Mustafa in Chapter 6, they rely on the label so they can speak out for the collective of refugees broadly understood. Malala, instead, chooses to include refugees' life stories in her collective storytelling enterprise but constantly reminds readers she is not one. What they share is being displaced. Dislocation, displacement, lack of belonging, those are the features shared by all of them.

The distinction is laid out at the same time the shared experience is outlined. Malala claims to have been displaced twice from a physical point of view: first, when she left Mingora for Shangla due to the war to be fought in the area between the Pakistani and allied forces and the Taliban, which turned her and her family into "IDPs – internally displaced persons" (Yousafzai 2019, 15); second, after the terrorist attack on her life, awakening from a coma in a UK hospital to find out she had "once again become displaced" (43). From a psychological point of view, the displacement does not only happen twice, but lasts a lifetime. To the trauma of losing one's home, other emotions are linked, namely shame and guilt. Asking others for help in such dire circumstances is accompanied by conflicting but unavoidable emotions: "To be displaced, on top of everything else, is to worry about being a burden on others" (24). In Malala's words, "*I am not a refugee*. But I understand the experience of being *displaced*, of having to leave my home, my country, because it has become too dangerous to remain" (45; emphasis added). Part 1 in her book is accurately entitled "*I Am* Displaced" (1–40; emphasis added). This piece of life writing intriguingly harks back to her memoir, *I Am Malala* (Yousafzai and Lamb 2013). It features the "I" of the activist, then claiming back her name and her individual identity, now effacing herself as one among many, as Part 2 is, following the book's premise, entitled "We Are Displaced" (Yousafzai 2019, 42–191). The "I" is thus subsumed into the collective pronoun and, from such a seemingly unimportant position, raises awareness for the many other "I"s that make up the "we." Identifying herself as a displaced person, Malala redirects public attention to one of the main social crises nowadays that, despite sheer numbers, has stopped featuring news headlines months ago and replaced by other issues, such as Brexit, which show a turn toward public attention on more local news and a move away from distant others. However, as Luc Boltanski (1999) would argue, distant suffering should urgently demand "commitment" (31) thus turning passive spectators into agents, moving them, beyond compassion, "to action" (Martínez García 2016, 127). Malala's book—just like the rest of her life-writing project—is an attempt to call on readers to be just that, ethical witnesses to a plight that, far from being over, is still raging.

In the Prologue displaced and refugees are brought together to raise awareness of the dehumanization they are suffering. Malala harnesses the data as she denounces the inadequacy of thinking in statistic terms alone. Their numbers are set in stark contrast with individual, "ordinary people" (Yousafzai 2019, xi)'s lives:

> For any refugee or any person displaced by violence, which is what most often makes people flee, it seems as if there is no safe place today. As of 2017, the United Nations counts 68.5 million people who were *forcibly displaced* worldwide, 25.4 million of which are considered refugees.
>
> The numbers are so staggering that you forget these are people *forced to leave* their homes. ... The displaced who make up these staggering numbers are *human beings* with hopes for a better future. (x; emphasis added)

Understanding the violence and dehumanization inherent to "forced displacement" is key to displaced people's activism for human rights (see Martínez García 2019b). Activists such as Nujeen Mustafa in Chapter 6 have openly denounced the emotional pain at being treated as numbers. All human rights activists, in this book and elsewhere, wish is to be treated as human beings, deserving of the same rights as any other person no matter their race, place, gender, or age.

Now 22, Malala Yousafzai has spent half her lifetime devoted to an activist cause, which in turn has become part and parcel of who she is. Her identity can no longer be understood without her fight for human rights.

Notes

1. I am indebted to Kate Douglas and Anna Poletti (2016) for their work on Malala Yousafzai's blog. See also Martínez García (2019a).
2. See Martínez García (2020) for further analysis of the technological affordances in Malala Yousafzai's online life-writing project.
3. I refer readers of this volume to Chapter 7, where I explore *On Her Shoulders* (Bombach 2018) the documentary on also-Nobel-Peace-Prize-winner Nadia Murad's life which precisely by avoiding direct talk or images of the

trauma endured realizes its goal—making audiences more readily empathize with her plight.

Works Cited

Ahmed, Beenish. 2014. What People in Pakistan Really Think About Nobel Prize Winner Malala Yousafzai. http://www.thinkprogress.org/world/2014/10/10/3578820/malala-yousafzai-nobel-prize/. Accessed 13 February 2020.

Alcoff, Linda Martín, and Laura Gray-Rosendale. 1996. Survivor Discourse: Transgression or Recuperation? In *Getting a Life: Everyday Uses of Autobiography*, ed. S. Smith and J. Watson, 198–225. Minneapolis: University of Minnesota Press.

Anon. 2009. Diary of a Pakistani Schoolgirl. *BBC News*, 19 January. http://news.bbc.co.uk/2/hi/south_asia/7834402.stm. Accessed 13 February 2020.

———. 2016. Best Sellers. *New York Times*, 12 June. https://www.nytimes.com/books/best-sellers/2016/06/12/?_r=0. Accessed 9 March 2017.

———. 2017a. Malala Yousafzai Named Youngest UN Messenger of Peace. *DW*, 10 April. http://www.dw.com/en/malala-yousafzai-named-youngest-un-messenger-of-peace/a-38375599. Accessed 23 May 2017.

———. 2017b. Amazon Best Sellers: Audible Audiobooks—Personal Memoirs. *Amazon*, 11 July. https://www.amazon.com/gp/bestsellers/books/2402218011/ref=zg_b_bs_2402218011_1. Accessed 11 July 2017.

———. 2017c. Amazon Best Sellers: Best Sellers in Women's Biographies. *Amazon*, 11 July. https://www.amazon.com/Best-Sellers-Books-Womens-Biographies/zgbs/books/2445. Accessed 11 July 2017.

———. 2017d. Amazon Best Sellers: Teen & Young Adult Social Activist Biographies. *Amazon*, 11 July. https://www.amazon.com/gp/bestsellers/books/10367684011/ref=zg_b_bs_10367684011_1. Accessed 11 July 2017.

Boltanski, Luc. 1999. *Distant Suffering: Morality, Media, and Politics*. Trans. Graham Burchell. Cambridge: Cambridge University Press.

Bombach, Alexandria. 2018. *On Her Shoulders*. Los Angeles, CA: RYOT Films.

boyd, danah. 2010. Social Network Sites as Networked Publics: Affordances, Dynamics, and Implications. In *A Networked Self: Identity, Community, and Culture on Social Network Sites*, ed. Zizi Papacharissi, 39–58. New York: Routledge.

Brown, Gordon. 2012. Malala Yousafzai's Courage Can Start New Movement for Global Education: Global Development. *The Guardian*, 25 October. https://www.theguardian.com/global-development/poverty-matters/2012/oct/25/malala-yousafzai-courage-global-education. Accessed 8 August 2017.

Chabba, Seerat. 2016. Malala Yousafzai Becomes Millionaire with Memoir Sales, Global Appearances. *International Business Times*, 30 June. http://www.ibt

imes.com/malala-yousafzai-becomes-millionaire-memoir-sales-global-appearances-2388405. Accessed 9 March 2017.
Douglas, Kate. 2017. Malala Yousafzai, Life Narrative and the Collaborative Archive. *Life Writing*, 14 (3): 297–311.
Douglas, Kate, and Anna Poletti. 2016. *Life Narratives and Youth Culture: Representation, Agency and Participation*. London: Palgrave Macmillan.
Ellick, Adam B. 2009. A Schoolgirl's Odyssey. YouTube, *New York Times*, 13 October. https://www.youtube.com/watch?v=a6T5DeZ9Z4c. Accessed 30 August 2015.
Ellick, Adam B., and Irfan Ashraf. 2009. Class Dismissed: The Death of Female Education. *New York Times*, Times Documentaries. http://www.nytimes.com/video/world/asia/100000001835296/class-dismissed.html. Accessed 30 August 2015.
Filipović, Zlata. 1995. *Zlata's Diary: A Child's Life in Sarajevo*. Trans. Christina Pribichevich-Zoric. London: Penguin.
Gidda, Mirren. 2017. Malala Yousafzai's New Mission: Can She Still Inspire as an Adult? *Newsweek*, 11 January. http://europe.newsweek.com/exclusive-malala-yousafzai-interview-davos-540978. Accessed 7 March 2017.
Gilmore, Leigh. 2017. Testimony. *a/b: Auto/Biography Studies* 32 (2): 307–309.
Guggenheim, Davis. 2015. *He Named Me Malala*. Abu Dhabi, United Arab Emirates: Image Nation Abu Dhabi.
Keen, Suzanne. 2016. Life Writing and the Empathetic Circle. *Concentric: Literary and Cultural Studies* 42 (2): 9–26.
Krznaric, Roman. 2014. *Empathy: A Handbook for Revolution*. London: Rider.
Malala Fund. 2014. Malala Yousafzai Nobel Peace Prize Speech. *YouTube*, 11 December. https://www.youtube.com/watch?v=MOqIotJrFVM. Accessed 13 February 2020.
———. 2017a. What We Do. https://www.malala.org. Accessed 7 March 2017.
———. 2017b. Malala Yousafzai's Statement on President Trump's Latest Executive Order on Refugees. *Facebook*, 27 January. https://www.facebook.com/MalalaFund/posts/1641249709222208. Accessed 8 March 2017.
——— (@MalalaFund). 2017c. Read Malala Yousafzai's Statement on President Trump's Executive Order on Refugees. *Twitter*, 27 January. https://twitter.com/malalafund/status/825101904116080647. Accessed 8 March 2017.
———. 2017d. Malala's Girl Power Trip. https://www.malala.org/trip. Accessed 8 August 2017.
———. 2019. YouTube Channel. *YouTube*. https://www.youtube.com/channel/UCk4FE7YqfCvSkhYal-yAx3Q. Accessed 12 March 2020.
———. 2020a. Gulmakai Network. https://malala.org/gulmakai-network. Accessed 13 February 2020.
———. 2020b. Assembly. https://assembly.malala.org/issue-archive. Accessed 13 February 2020.

——— (@MalalaFund). 2020c. *Twitter*. https://twitter.com/MalalaFund. Accessed 12 March 2020.

——— (@MalalaFund). 2020d. *Facebook*. https://es-la.facebook.com/MalalaFund/. Accessed 12 March 2020.

——— (@MalalaFund). 2020e. *Instagram*. https://www.instagram.com/malalafund/?hl=es. Accessed 12 March 2020.

Martínez García, Ana Belén. 2016. Narrative Emotions and Human Rights Life Writing. In *On the Move: Glancing Backwards to Build a Future in English Studies*, ed. Aitor Ibarrola-Armendariz and Jon Ortiz de Urbina Arruabarrena, 127–132. Bilbao: University of Deusto.

———. 2019a. Construction and Collaboration in Life-Writing Projects: Malala Yousafzai's Activist 'I'. *Journal of Writing in Creative Practice* 12 (1–2): 201–217.

———. 2019b. Denouncing Human Trafficking in China: North Korean Women's Memoirs as Evidence. *State Crime Journal* 8 (1): 59–79.

———. 2019c. Empathy for Social Justice: The Case of Malala Yousafzai. *Journal of English Studies* 17: 253–275.

———. 2020. Women Activists' Strategies of Online Self-Presentation. *AI & Society: Journal of Knowledge, Culture and Communication*. Special Issue on Iteration as Persuasion in a Digital World.

Media Centre. 2017. BBC Radio 3 Announces 2017 International Women's Day Programming. *BBC*, 27 January. http://www.bbc.co.uk/mediacentre/latestnews/2017/bbc-radio-3-international-womens-day-programming. Accessed 10 March 2017.

Melancon, Nicole. 2012. I Am Malala: A Crusader for Girls' Education Worldwide. *Huffington Post*, 9 November. http://www.huffingtonpost.com/nicole-melancon/malala-yousafzai-girls-education_b_2080502.html. Accessed 9 March 2017.

Mukhopadhyay, Samitha. 2019. Malala Yousafzai on Education, Islamophobia, and the New Wave of Youth Activism. *Teen Vogue*, 16 December. https://www.teenvogue.com/story/malala-yousafzai-education-islamophobia-teen-girls. Accessed 13 February 2020.

Radio 3. 2017. International Women's Day: Speak Out. Recital, *BBC*, 8 March. http://www.bbc.co.uk/programmes/b08hcfkm. Accessed 10 March 2017.

Rao, Mallika. 2015. Why Do Some Pakistanis Hate Malala So Much? *Huffington Post*, 9 October. http://www.huffingtonpost.com/entry/why-do-pakistanis-hate-Malala_56174cede4b0e66ad4c74739. Accessed 13 February 2020.

Simonsen, Karen-Margrethe, and Jonas Ross Kjaergård (eds.). 2017. *Discursive Framings of Human Rights: Agency and Victimhood*. Abingdon: Birkbeck Law Press.

Slaughter, Joseph R. 2009. Humanitarian Reading. In *Humanitarianism and Suffering: The Mobilization of Empathy*, ed. Richard Ashby Wilson and Richard D. Brown, 88–107. New York: Cambridge University Press.

Smith, Sidonie. 2006. Narratives and Rights: *Zlata's Diary* and the Circulation of Stories of Suffering Ethnicity. *WSQ: Women's Studies Quarterly* 34 (1–2): 133–152.

Smith, Sidonie, and Julia Watson. 2010. *Reading Autobiography: A Guide for Interpreting Life Narratives*. 2nd ed. Minneapolis: Minnesota University Press.

———. 2012. Witness or False Witness?: Metrics of Authenticity, Collective I-Formations, and the Ethic of Verification in First-Person Testimony. *Biography* 35 (4): 590–626.

———. 2017. *Life Writing in the Long Run: A Smith & Watson Autobiography Studies Reader*. Ann Arbor, MI: Maize.

Sutton, Karolina. 2017. Malala Yousafzai—I Am Malala. *Curtis Brown*. https://www.curtisbrown.co.uk/client/malala-yousafzai/work/i-am-malala. Accessed 9 March 2017.

United Nations. 2013. Malala Yousafzai Addresses United Nations Youth Assembly. *YouTube*, 13 July. https://www.youtube.com/watch?v=3rNhZu3ttIU. Accessed 12 March 2020.

———. 2015. Malala Yousafzai—Call to Action. *YouTube*, 25 September. https://www.youtube.com/watch?v=qEswHDTMdck. Accessed 14 February 2020.

———. 2017. Malala Yousafzai (UN Messenger of Peace) Conversation About Girls' Education. *YouTube*, 10 April. https://www.youtube.com/watch?v=b5FzjqAIT60. Accessed 14 February 2020.

Whitley, Kate. 2017. Speak Out: An Inspirational New Work Based on Words by Malala. *BBC Radio 3*, 9 March. http://www.bbc.co.uk/programmes/p04w9363. Accessed 10 March 2017.

Whitlock, Gillian. 2007. *Soft Weapons: Autobiography in Transit*. Chicago: University of Chicago Press.

———. 2015. *Postcolonial Life Narratives: Testimonial Transactions*. Oxford: Oxford University Press.

Yousafzai, Malala. 2019. *We Are Displaced: My Journey and Stories from Refugee Girls Around the World*. London: Weidenfeld & Nicolson.

——— (@Malala). 2020a. *Twitter*. https://twitter.com/malala. Accessed 12 March 2020.

——— (@malala). 2020b. *Instagram*. https://www.instagram.com/malala/?hl=es. Accessed 12 March 2020.

Yousafzai, Malala, and Christina Lamb. 2013. *I Am Malala: The Girl Who Stood Up for Education and Was Shot by the Taliban*. London: Weidenfeld & Nicolson.

Yousafzai, Malala, and Patricia McCormick. 2014. *I Am Malala: How One Girl Stood Up for Education and Changed the World*. London: Little, Brown.

CHAPTER 3

Hyeonseo Lee: Seeking Justice for the North Korean People on TED.com

Abstract This chapter looks at how Hyeonseo Lee imbricates personal memory and collective suffering in her life-writing activism. She has become a spokesperson for North Koreans at both national and international levels, giving public talks where she explains hardships she endured and witnessed. In 2013, TED.com released Lee's talk. The instability of US-DPRK relations at the time made it an instant sensation, which proves life writing is inseparable from politics. The interplay of offline and online self-construction expands the notion of what used to be separate realms but have become one entangled narrative. Her memoir profited from the viral TED talk and vice versa. Deploying social media for human rights activism, Lee's life writing succeeds in raising awareness for a collective via multimodal means of self-expression.

Keywords Hyeonseo Lee · Life-writing activism · North Korea · Witnessing · TED.com · Offline/online

Born in Hyesan, North Korea, in January 1980, Hyeonseo Lee is the oldest of the young women whose life-writing activist projects are commented on in the present volume. She shares with Yeonmi Park (Chapter 4) the fact that they were both born in the same village, but their social class was different, as were the historical times they had to live, which helps explain why their memoirs do not read that much alike. Hyeonseo Lee escaped North Korea at 17, did not reach South Korea

A. B. Martínez García, *New Forms of Self-Narration*, Palgrave Studies in Life Writing, https://doi.org/10.1007/978-3-030-46420-2_3

until she was 28, did not lead a public life until she was 30 (Lee and John 2015, 288), did not publish her memoir until she was 35. Despite taking so long to come forward as an activist for the rights of North Koreans, she has become one of the faces[1] one associates with precisely that, mostly thanks to two vital factors—her viral TED talk (Lee 2013) and her best-selling memoir (Lee and John 2015). Both texts, as will be seen in what follows, constitute part of her life-writing project in which she emerges as a human rights activist in the public sphere over the past few years.

Imbricating Personal Memory and Collective Suffering

Unlike many other famous defectors, when Hyeonseo Lee left North Korea, she did so willingly but not for political reasons. She was just a 17-year-old girl who wanted to experience life outside her country before crossing the border was considered a crime upon her coming of age. She herself acknowledges her naïveté in her memoir, where she looks back at a past of ideological indoctrination that did not allow her to see that her situation was other than normal (Martínez García 2017a, 588). It took Lee over 10 years in China to finally reach South Korea, where she started learning English at a very rapid pace. The enthusiasm for the new language and admittedly her good looks are key to her fast becoming a spokesperson for North Koreans first at a national level, soon at an international level, giving public talks where she explains the hardships she endured and witnessed.[2] The deployment of "strategic narrative empathy" (Keen 2016) can be tracked in all her interventions, offline and online, on platforms like Facebook or Twitter, where she started posting at 32. This seemingly older age in comparison with other young women activists in this volume (Chapters 2, 4, 5, 6, and 7) does not detract from the impact her girlhood memories may have upon reader/audience. This is in line with the complicity between taking up testimonial life writing empathetically and a "'primed' readership" for such stories (Whitlock 2007, 13) that vouches for what many have described as a "memoir boom" (see Rak 2013).

In what follows, building on previous work (Martínez García 2017a, 2018, 2019),[3] I trace Hyeonseo Lee's "I" of the girl victim of human rights transgressions, the "I" of the witness, and the collective nature of the pronoun. Lee's experience, even if personal, is emblematic of the plight of many other North Koreans, both in her age and to date. How she navigates the tensions between the personal and the collective is key to understanding her story in terms of testimonial life writing. The narrating "I" claims the right to tell her own story, but it is an "I" poignantly calling attention to ongoing ethical—and legal—violations. Lee deploys the accusatory narrative stance typical of testimonial accounts (Couser 2012, 41) to emphasize school indoctrination. Thus, when Lee remembers being six and attending kindergarten, she suggests the profound change that affected her family relationship: "In a sense, I no longer belonged to them. I belonged to the state" (Lee and John 2015, 20). In this passage, much as in the rest of her life-writing project, "The 'I' occupies the position of the victim, retracing memories that are individual as well as collective, since the experience of losing one's sense of family affected all schoolchildren" (Martínez García 2017a, 589). As part of North Koreans' cultural memory, Lee's memories are imbued by historical significance as well as affect (Schaffer and Smith 2004, 9). The "architectures of memory" (9) allow Lee to reconstruct the process of ideological indoctrination she went through at school. In this regard, she is quite explicit in her public accusation of the regime: "Ideological indoctrination began on the first day" (Lee and John 2015, 21). Examples include the attempts on the part of the authorities to rewrite history (see Seth 2010, 138; Oh and Hassig 2000, 25), which the adult Lee denounces: "The past was not set in stone, and was occasionally rewritten" (Lee and John 2015, 49). In Schaffer and Smith's (2004) words, her comments are an attempt at inscribing "counter-histories" (17) and so at "changing the official narrative" (Martínez García 2017a, 593). Her adult defiance of myths surrounding the enemies of the state, namely Americans, Japanese, and Chinese, serves to witness to the "brainwashing education" children had to endure (593).

As posited in a recent article for *State Crime Journal*, North Korean women's memoirs may well be read as testimonial narratives denouncing human trafficking in China (Martínez García 2019). Lee's memoir is not the most-detailed account of trafficking, as she does not claim to have suffered it herself. Rather, she recounts several episodes where she nearly fell prey to such networks but managed to escape. One such instance happens when she is living in Shenyang, a place that appears sordidly depicted in other memoirists' recollections (see Park 2015, 173–183). Lee recalls being offered a job at a "hair salon" with "'therapy rooms' with smoked-glass doors" (Lee and John 2015, 124) and "the filthiest room I had seen in my life" (125). Luckily, Lee escapes before any physical abuse takes place (126). And yet, Lee's eye-witnessing "I," in describing the dreadful conditions of the salon and how others were forced to stay, compels readers to be witnesses to those other North Korean girls and women who are trafficked and cannot escape. As noted by Julia Watson (2016), "The eyewitness holds a special status in narrative accounts. The attestation 'I was there' makes a unique bid for readers' attention and empathy" (683). Lee's memoir, like similar memoirs, is "an attempt at invoking the victimized other of the trafficked girl/woman in both context-specific and universal terms" (Martínez García 2019, 72). This is in line with Suzanne Keen's (2016) thesis that combining an account of ethnic victimization—deploying ambassadorial strategic empathy (20)—with universalizing claims—deploying broadcast strategic empathy (22)—makes for a more impactful and long-lasting narrative (22).

Besides speaking for those women without a voice (Martínez García 2019, 63), Lee witnesses to other trafficked people's experiences, including that of her family. Lee's experience of and with traffickers is seen to emphasize the risks North Koreans are willing to incur in escaping their country to reach freedom. The description of how these brokers operate paints an ugly picture of a reality for many undocumented migrants. Without being granted the status of refugees, as this narrative shows, North Koreans are subject to forcible repatriations every step of the way, but also to imprisonment and fines, as well as to physical and psychological abuse (see Martínez García 2019).

Though Lee had been living in South Korea for a while, it is precisely when her family arrives that she takes a more proactive role as an ambassador for North Koreans' rights, joining PSCORE (People for Successful COrean REunification) (Lee and John 2015, 186), a "Non-profit NGO based in Seoul, South Korea, working towards reunification and assisting North Korean defectors" (PSCORE 2017). With her subsequent engagement in the public sphere, Lee reflects on her role in shaping people's perceptions of North Koreans, fighting against the dominating stereotypes in the media:

> Slowly, I started speaking out in defence of defectors, and about the human rights abuses in North Korea – first, in defector group meetings, then in small public speeches, then on a new television show called *Now on My Way to Meet You*, in which all the guests were female defectors, given new clothes in vibrant colours to dispel public perceptions of North Koreans as

shabby and pitiful. The show had a big impact in transforming attitudes in South Korea towards defectors. (Lee and John 2015, 288)

It is interesting to note that Yeonmi Park, who will be the subject of the following chapter in this volume (Chapter 4), also appeared on the same South Korean TV show.

But central to Lee's becoming a well-known activist on behalf of North Koreans was her TED talk (2013). Thanks to her speaking out on minor events, some of them TEDx ones, she was "chosen through a worldwide talent search to give a talk at a TED conference" (Lee and John 2015, 290) in California.

Understanding the Viral Phenomenon of Her TED Talk

In 2013, TED.com released Hyeonseo Lee's talk on their platform. Entitled "My Escape from North Korea" (Lee 2013), it amasses a total 14,129,732 views so far on TED and is therefore, among the many other TED-related events she has been involved in (2012, 2015a, b), her most famous "visual/verbal life narrative" (Smith and Watson 2002, 352). The instability of US-DPRK relations at that moment made it an instant sensation. The context is of paramount importance, considering the escalation of tension between the two countries in 2013. On 22 January 2013, the United Nations Security Council passed Resolution 2087 (UNSC 2013), condemning North Korea's 12 December 2012 rocket launch and expanding economic sanctions (BBC 2013a). In retaliation, just two days later North Korean authorities announced a new nuclear weapon and long-range missile test, threatening the United States of America as their primary target (BBC 2013b). After carrying out said test the following day, the European Union added further sanctions (Croft 2013). On 19 February, at a United Nations meeting in Geneva, North Korea threatened the "final destruction" of South Korea (BBC 2013c). On 7 March, the North extended the threat of a nuclear strike to the United States (Kim and Charbonneau 2013). The following months saw a heated exchange between world leaders and the North Korean regime, with almost daily updates on one remark or another with North Korean leader Kim Jong-un using rhetoric of violent retribution against the West, including South Korea and Japan.

With the visibility gained after the TED talk delivered in February 2013, Lee was later "invited to New York to testify before the United Nations Commission of Enquiry on Human Rights in North Korea, alongside some defectors who had survived the North Korean gulag" (Lee and John 2015, 290). On her website (Lee 2019c), one notices two key venues where she gave public testimony in 2014: at the Committee for Human Rights in North Korea (HRNK) in Washington, DC, and at the UN Security Council in New York. Lee's testimony and outspokenness finally brought her to the attention of the North Korean regime. At the same time as the UN Commission declared North Korea was committing "violations that may amount to crimes against humanity" (UN COI 2014a, 3),[4] Lee was labeled one of a group of "criminals" and "terrorists" by the North Korean Central News Agency (Lee and John 2015, 290). Her public testimony may have influenced policy change, as with other young women activists' testimony before the United Nations.

All these tensions, for better or worse, explain why the TED talk was so popular at the time it was published online. The peak of attention, however, would take several years. This was in the year 2017, a point in which the tensions between North Korea and the United States reached a climax. To nuclear and missile tests, the United States and South Korea responded with a joint military exercise in August 2017, as well as tweeting threats, mainly on the part of US President Donald Trump. A further nuclear test in September made people fear impending war. At this point in time, with a renewed surge in public interest in the Korean peninsula, the TED talk became a viral phenomenon (Martínez García 2018).

Yet, what followed that period of unrest were sudden eased relations, with North Korea resuming talks with the South and even agreeing to participate in the 2018 Winter Olympics in a joint Korean team. An unprecedented bilateral summit between Kim and Trump was held in Singapore on 12 June 2018. It resulted in a joint declaration calling for the "complete denuclearization of the Korean peninsula" (White House 2018b). But those apparent advances were halted after a second summit between Kim and Trump in Hanoi, Vietnam, on 27 February 2019 ended abruptly. The instability and high unpredictability of these two leaders would help explain the virality of the TED talk, which owes much to the "technological and affective affordances" of Twitter (Martínez García 2017b, 145). Thus, heightened cycles of attention around the topic of

North Korea serve to address the potential reasons behind the talk again coming to the fore in recent times.

As seen in the previous case study (Chapter 2) and in future Chapters (4, 5, 6, 7), life writing is inseparable from politics, particularly when it is a conscious form of activism. Human rights activism is at its most impactful when it is a "first-person account of suffering" (Whitlock 2015, 16) or of "victimization" (76). Despite its critics, such life writing deserves a more thorough analysis than the attention it has received so far.

Reading TED Talk and Memoir Side by Side

The memoir (Lee and John 2015) has profited from the viral TED talk (Lee 2013) as much as vice versa, with readers taking an interest in Lee's public speeches, interviews, and articles. The continuous crossing of textual mode supplements general interest not just in her story but in the broader picture of North Koreans and how they may or may not be living. As in the former case of Malala Yousafzai (Chapter 2), Lee's life writing succeeds in raising awareness for a collective via multimodal means of self-expression (Smith and Watson 2010, 167–192) and authorial strategic narrative empathizing techniques (Keen 2016). In my article on "TED Talks as Life Writing" for the journal *Life Writing* (Martínez García 2018), I conducted a close reading of Lee's (2013) TED talk in relation to Park's (2014) TEDx talk. However, no comparison was drawn between these TED talks and the corresponding memoirs. In what follows, I read Lee's TED talk (2013) and memoir (Lee and John 2015) side by side.

In her viral TED talk, Lee (2013) refuses to give details either about how she escaped North Korea or what happened in China. This might have been, on the one hand, due to a potential copyright agreement that would have prevented her from disclosing what she had written about in her memoir (Lee and John 2015), forthcoming at the time. Or, on the other hand, she might have wanted to make viewers wish to buy the book to know more. Conversely, readers of her memoir in 2015 were drawn to this and other speeches, as well as interviews, which populate the Internet and social media. The fact that a TED speaker focuses on a partial account, or a single event, is nothing new. Instead, it is a strategy to try to capture the audience's attention in over 12 minutes, aiming to convey a story that has an impact, notably emotional impact, and this in line with human rights activism, to garner support for a social justice cause (Martínez García 2018).

No longer the teenager she was when the transgressions she discusses took place, Lee cannot claim the voice of a young girl or pretend to invoke pity on the sole grounds of her looks.[5] She therefore constructs her argument as a narrative of coming of age, but, as Kate Douglas and Anna Poletti (2016) suggest when discussing Emmanuel Jal's *War Child*, one that represents "a coming to knowledge through trauma" (100). Lee (2013) relates how she grew up in North Korea, the progressive changes in her life, and how she has come to be the person she is. Much as the regime remains one of the most closed in the world, the audience is well aware of an ingrained hatred against Westerners which Lee explicitly addresses at the beginning of her talk, when she says that she "never learned much about the outside world, except that America, South Korea, Japan are the enemies." Her English is not very good, as she had to learn when she was already a grown-up woman. In her memoir, she claims that she decided to learn English at 28 because it is "the world's common language" (Lee and John 2015, 261).

Lee's efforts to speak in public must be read as attempts to reach across the cultural and geopolitical divides and communicate her message to a global audience. Even in broken English, she manages to convey her ideas. In fact, this is not the first event in which she has participated, which explains why she does not seem too nervous while struggling for words. Lee's (2013) TED talk is structured following a common storyline for Western audiences, the rags-to-riches story, a strategy that some postcolonial critics have seen as a method for deprived subjects to inscribe themselves in global culture and reclaim agency (Moore-Gilbert 2009, 15).[6] Lee wields the first-person singular pronoun strategically, pointedly so in the title of the talk: This is not the story of any other North Korean, but hers and hers only. Throughout her life-writing text, read closely, the "I" features prominently, with over 60 mentions in less than 15 minutes. But this "I" goes from childhood into adulthood in the space of some minutes. First, it is the "I" of a little girl: "When I was little, I thought my country was the best on the planet" (Lee 2013). The opening line in her speech sets the scene for the harsh events Lee was forced to witness as a child: "When I was seven years old, I saw my first public execution. But I thought my life in North Korea was normal." Her memories of that moment are devoid of emotion, as she acknowledges that it was part of everyday normal life in North Korea. Nevertheless, a letter from a woman close to death due to extreme food deprivation is what sets her wondering about justice in her country. Lee solicits a compassionate reading of her text, close to tears while relating that episode that first "shocked" her. From that moment on, Lee looks at death with different eyes, more aware and critical of what she sees:

> when I was walking past a train station, I saw something terrible that to this day I can't erase from my memory. A lifeless woman was lying on the ground, while an emaciated child in her arms just stared helplessly at his mother's face. But nobody helped them … Sometimes, I saw dead bodies floating down the river.

Interestingly, Lee insists on invoking the voice of a girl to speak of her time in China, claiming that "it was hard living as a young girl without my family" (2013), though readers of her memoir know she was already 17 by the time she left North Korea (Lee and John 2015, 92). The reason behind this insistence on her being just a girl may be an ultimate call for empathic identification that has long been assigned to young women in the tradition of the diarist Anne Frank (Douglas and Poletti 2016, 20–22). If she is perceived as a vulnerable subject on the grounds of gender and age, as Sidonie Smith (2006) argues of Zlata Filipović, the audience is more likely to empathize with the narrator's plight as "a 'universal' voice of the child suffering from human rights abuses" (152).[7]

From a life that is made of individual feats of courage, Lee suddenly realizes not everything is possible on her own. Thus, when her family is detained in Laos until she pays a bribe and having run out of money, she has to rely on the kindness of a stranger, who listens to her and pays for their release:

> I thanked him with all my heart, and I asked him, 'Why are you helping me?'
>
> 'I'm not helping you,' he said. 'I'm helping the North Korean people.' (Lee 2013)

The radical act of kindness of this stranger marks a turning point in Lee's life and in her life-writing text. As if awakened to the realization that her story is not just her own, but the story of many other North Koreans seeking to escape their country's oppressive regime, in the remaining part of her speech one can note a change away from the individual victim/survivor voice and toward the collective awareness-raising voice. All of a sudden, she is one among many North Koreans, one member of a community, "we North Korean people": "The kind stranger symbolized new hope for me and the North Korean people, when we needed it most. And he showed me that the kindness of strangers and the support of the international community are truly the rays of hope *we North Korean people* need" (Lee 2013; emphasis added). The nuanced repetition of "kind stranger" and "hope" present Lee's concluding thoughts and final aim. With her emotional discourse, she is reaching out to other "kind strangers" who can contribute to her cause. She connects asking for help to the idea of "hope," calling forth the ethics of humanitarianism. Aware that the key to changing the situation of North Koreans is outside their control, Lee (2013) invokes the "international community" twice, finishing her intervention by referring to the "international support" they need to prosper. This kind of discourse is problematic. As noted by Sidonie Smith and Julia Watson (2017), it is the typical humanitarian reading associated with global aid campaigns which turn victims in need of help into commodities. Like Smith and Watson, I strive to get past notions of victimhood and agency, and reformulate the complex negotiations of the two, redefining what a subject is by looking at how she writes herself.

Lee's memoir is, as the title suggests—*The Girl with Seven Names* (Lee and John 2015), an attempt at reconstructing her identity after years of psychic fragmentation. She recounts the experience of changing her name up to seven times for many different reasons. This is the central issue in the book, and much of it revolves around the various phases in her life, and the need to hide or to pretend something that she is not to the point that it was to recover herself and heal over time. Though North Korea features in the second half of the title—*A North Korean Defector's Story* (Lee and John 2015), the time spent on criticizing the regime is much less than in other defectors' memoirs. Why is that, in direct contradiction to its title? Because Lee chooses to describe her inner turmoil instead. Only after one finishes reading the memoir does one realize that the reason for her constant terror of being identified is inherited from a childhood of indoctrination. Her fear of being recognized and sent back to North Korea is what pushes her to keep changing her name over and over again. More poignant details of crimes endured and political statements denouncing those are found elsewhere. In Lee's memoir, however, one finds an "I" struggling to cope with her past, trying to come to terms with all the stages in her life, reconstructing a fragmented identity and giving it coherence with the benefit of hindsight.

The narrative is chronologically oriented for readers to better understand Lee's life story. Importantly, not all the name changes are in fear of government retaliation as she would later observe in retrospect. And yet, it is precisely at the time of her TED talk that she chooses to start the narrative. Lee's introduction (Lee and John 2015) begins by explaining her current name as she is about to speak before the TED auditorium in Long Beach, California:

> My name is Hyeonseo Lee.
>
> It is not the name I was born with, nor one of the names forced on me, at different times, by circumstance. But it is the one I gave myself, once I'd reached freedom. Hyeon means sunshine. Seo means good fortune. I chose it so that I would live my life in light and warmth, and not return to the shadow. (XI)

That Lee chose to start the book from the standpoint of the TED talk in 2013, not from the present in 2015, is a manifesto to the interrelatedness of the two texts in creating her activist identity. If she has endured an identity crisis for most of her life, the TED talk is the single event her newly formed identity hinges upon just as Malala Yousafzai's identity was reconstructed after the attack on her life (see Chapter 2). Moreover, the *Bildungsroman* in the narrative, suggested in my reading of Lee's TED talk above (see Martínez García 2018), is here specifically pointed out in her own words: "As I read back through this book, I see that it is a story of my awakening, a long and difficult *coming of age*. I have come to accept that as a North Korean defector I am an outsider in the world. An exile" (Lee and John 2015, XII; emphasis added). The memoir, according to Lee's introductory remarks, would not have been published had it not been for the TED talk.

TED talk and memoir share the following human rights-related themes: indoctrination, hunger, and human trafficking. But they diverge in the memoir's detailed explanation of how Lee moved out of one identity and into the next, adopting a different stance at every turn. The title of the memoir, *The Girl with Seven Names* (Lee and John 2015) is thus vouched for and teased out. After describing various name changes accompanied all the while by a strong identity crisis, it is not until she wishes to apply for university that she changes her name one last time. Far from doing so because of fear of potential retaliation of the North Korean regime, she does it because "a name change would bring better luck" (Lee and John 2015, 218). Therefore, she visits a professional name-giver who gives her a choice of 5 names, out of which "I chose Hyeon-seo" (219). Then, she does not heed the advice of the fortune teller, who warns her it may be too strong a name and she should take a nickname: "*No*, I thought. *No more names. Hyeonseo it is*" (219). Lee has certainly refused to give it up ever since.

Deploying Social Media for Human Rights Activism

YouTube has played an important role in Hyeonseo Lee's becoming known as an activist. With links to interviews and public speeches on her personal website (Lee 2019b), as well as on platforms such as Twitter and Facebook, the YouTube videos are spread further than if only one of these social media were used (Papacharissi 2012). With over 2 billion users across the world, YouTube is a key platform of dissemination. The easiness by which comments may be posted, likes and dislikes chosen, and a total number of views on display, all go to affirm the power of technological affordances for advocacy and activism. YouTube works hand in hand with all the other platforms, contributing to a particular video becoming viral, as the link can be retweeted, liked or part of a new post on any or all of those. A good example might be the TED talk discussed earlier (Lee 2013). This collaboration helps to co-construct a message, and, in the case of human rights activists, a YouTube video may even be read as part of their life-writing project—indeed, a co-constructed testimony (see Chapter 2; Gilmore 2017b).

In an interview with Fox News reporter Greg Palkot for Special Report, Lee admits to having cried out of happiness after Trump's rhetoric against Kim during the spring of 2017: "No … President said the words until today … even though we have suffered for seven decades" (Palkot 2017). At that point, the promise of a potential attack that would remove Kim from power is perceived as a solution to the suffering of her people.

Lee went on to meet US President Donald Trump, a meeting she first advertised on Facebook (Lee 2018d) and later on Twitter (Lee 2018a). Lee's tweets, if read on a timeline, navigate the tensions between US politics and international politics, but there is an overall sense of trying to be present in those situations where potential geopolitical decisions are shaped.

On 2 February 2018, Lee was one among the chosen North Korean defectors meeting US President Donald Trump in the Oval Office at the White House. One by one, they all told their story to the president and the media. When it was her turn, Lee introduced herself as "the author of *The Girl with Seven Names*" and a person from "the most ridiculous country on earth" (White House 2018a). She then thanked Trump for saying that "the US will act alone on North Korea if China does not help. That made me cry, because that is exactly what I'd wanted to hear for so long from leaders like you" (White House 2018a). This promise of potential violence against the regime has been avoided by most presidents, who preferred to avoid confrontation, most notably former US President Barack Obama during his presidency. With Trump, a rhetoric of confrontation is expected, particularly in his virulent tweets and his public appearances. Lee praises one such speech: "You put the spotlight on North Korean human rights issues in front of the entire South Korean National Assembly and refreshed the attention on this kind of issue so I cannot thank you enough" (White House 2018a). As will be seen in the following chapter on Yeonmi Park (Chapter 4), this praise of and gratefulness toward Trump is not shared by other North Korean defector-activists, who think his words are not enough. Importantly, Trump has since evolved from a rhetoric of violence to a rapprochement, being the first US President in history to meet with a North Korean leader, not only once but twice, as commented on above. However, Lee could not know these developments at the time of their meeting. Instead, Lee made a public plea where she denounced China as much as North Korea due to their policy of "refoulement,"[8] though not using the legal term: "Please help us stop the repatriations from China and give the North Korean people the freedom that they deserve" (White House 2018a). Lee ended her speech by presenting President Trump with a copy of her book. The following day, Lee enthusiastically tweeted about Trump's support for her book: "President #Trump said #TheGirlwithSevenNames it's an amazing title and he will read it" (@HyeonseoLeeNK, 3 Feb. 2018). Meanwhile, Trump was quickly setting up a meeting to discuss North Korea and take action: "I will be meeting with Henry Kissinger at 1:45 p.m. Will be discussing North Korea, China and the Middle East" (@realDonaldTrump, 8 Feb. 2018, 10:44). That Lee appears on the photographs posted by Vice President Michael Pence (@V7VOA, 8 Feb. 2018; @VP, 9

Feb. 2018) is quite telling. Her presence at those key events promotes the image of Lee as representative of the North Korean people and might well imbue her with an aura of prestige which contributes to more readers of her memoirs and more viewers of her talk, as well as earns her more followers on social media. However, Lee's decision to come across as pro-Trump is quite significant. From then on, Lee will not be part of other activists' campaigns against Trump's policies. Lee's decision to align herself politically with the Republican Party, with her veiled criticism of earlier presidencies, sets her apart from most North Korean defectors, most notably Yeonmi Park (Chapter 4). Lee even tweeted a photograph where she is seen together with a smiling Trump, thanking him for his support: "I really appreciate that #President #Trump took the time to meet with #NorthKorean escapees to hear our stories and discuss important issues. It means a lot that the President cares about us" (@HyeonseoLeeNK, 8 Mar. 2018). Her use of emotional language strongly suggests her intention of connecting with him further. Lee's strategic deployment of an "ethics of care" (Slote 2007) is important in two ways: First, she links caring with empathy, which is the key concept all human rights activism pivots around; second, by making Trump seem relatable, in his words and in his smile, she is arguably supporting his politics too.[9]

In an interview for Channel 4 in March 2018, Lee confessed "I never thought this time [the] North Korean regime [would] actually ask [for] the summit between the two leaders this fast … never expected" (Lee 2018b). As will be seen in the following chapter, Trump's policy toward North Korea and his decision to meet with Kim was not as welcome by other defectors, most notably Yeonmi Park (Chapter 4), who even set up her own YouTube channel to comment on the Trump-Kim meeting. Soon after that first meeting, however, Lee herself expressed her skepticism regarding its outcomes, speaking at Forbes Women's Summit about the unlikelihood of North Korea's denuclearization (@Forbes, 19 June 2018).

Yet, since November 2018, Lee seems to have stopped her activity on Twitter (Lee 2018a) to apparently focus on her posts on Facebook (Lee 2018d) with the very same handle—@HyeonseoLeeNK. However, her posts on the latter platform have also stopped since July 2019. In preparation for the second Trump-Kim meeting, Lee seems to have been interested in the potential rapprochement between the United States and the DPRK, promoted by the Trump administration. For example, she used Facebook to publicize her opinion piece written for the *New York Times* on 3 December 2018 (Lee 2018c), in which she argued in favor of Korean reunification, which is clearly in line with the Trump-Kim summits rationale. On Facebook, that post garners 1812 likes as of 31 January 2020 (Lee 2018d). Perhaps Lee stopped using Twitter due to trolling threats, or because it is easier to connect to similar-minded people or opinion groups on Facebook. But whether Lee will again tweet or post remains a mystery, much as there are no news regarding the collective memoir and NGO she was said to be preparing since 2016 (Lee 2019a).

Notes

1. As Kay Schaffer and Sidonie Smith (2004) argue, first-person human rights life narratives put "a human face to suffering" (3). In turn, becoming the face that stands for a collective of disadvantaged others is of uppermost importance if activists are to successfully mobilize empathy (Wilson and Brown 2009, 2).
2. This use of English and beauty to access the global public sphere is posited in this volume as strategies for young women activists (Chapters 2, 4, 5, 7). It is a double-edged sword, potentially commodifying women, but also obtaining support for their causes.
3. This chapter is derived in part from an article published in *a/b: Auto/Biography Studies* (2017) © The Autobiography Society, available online: https://www.tandfonline.com/doi/abs/10.1080/08989575.2017.1338004; an article published in *Life Writing* (2018) © Taylor & Francis, available online: https://www.tandfonline.com/doi/full/10.1080/14484528.2017.1405317; and an article published in *State Crime Journal* (2019) © Pluto Journals, available online: https://www.jstor.org/stable/10.13169/statecrime.8.1.0059.
4. For an expanded overview on those "crimes against humanity," see the full report (UN COI 2014b).
5. The discussion of Lee's (2013) TED Talk was previously published as part of an article in the journal *Life Writing* © Taylor & Francis (Martínez García 2018, 491–493). It has been updated and expanded with permission from the publishers.
6. The "rags-to-riches" frame has, however, been vehemently criticized by other life-writing scholars like Leigh Gilmore (2017a), who sees it as a neoliberal tool matching "the rhetoric of self-improvement ... that functions as vernacular corollary to democracy in the United States" (91).
7. This universal child's voice may also be read as a strategic narrative empathizing technique, calling on the audience to think back to their own childhood. In Keen's (2016) terms, the narrating "I" is here deploying

both "broadcast" empathy (22)—standing for a child out of place and out of time, a universal child whose life is endangered—but also "ambassadorial" empathy (20)—a North Korean child, representative of a community of repressed others radically different from the audience, made up of Americans.

8. Article 33(1) of the Refugee Convention states: "No Contracting State shall expel or return ('refouler') a refugee in any manner whatsoever to the frontiers of territories where his life or freedom would be threatened on account of his race, religion, nationality, membership of a particular social group or political opinion" (UNHCR 2010, 30). As argued by Kurlantzick and Mason (2006), China contravenes the Convention by repatriating North Koreans without prior screening. See Martínez García (2019) for further information.
9. Discussing empathy and relatability, Suzanne Keen states in life-writing settings the latter (2016, 12) is transcended by attending to narrative emotions as inherent "forms of affect" (2015, 152).

Works Cited

BBC. 2013a. UN Extends North Korea Sanctions Over Rocket Launch. *BBC News*, 22 January. https://www.bbc.co.uk/news/world-asia-21137136. Accessed 31 January 2020.

———. 2013b. North Korea "Plans Third Nuclear Test." *BBC News*, 24 January. https://www.bbc.co.uk/news/world-asia-21175466. Accessed 31 January 2020.

———. 2013c. North Korea Threatens "Final Destruction" of South Korea. *BBC News*, 19 February. https://www.bbc.co.uk/news/world-asia-21510479. Accessed 31 January 2020.

Couser, G. Thomas. 2012. *Memoir: An Introduction*. Oxford: Oxford University Press.

Croft, Adrian. 2013. EU to Tighten Sanctions on North Korea After Nuclear Test. *Reuters*, 16 February. https://uk.reuters.com/article/us-korea-north-eu/eu-to-tighten-sanctions-on-north-korea-after-nuclear-test-idUKBRE91E0VZ20130216?mod=related&channelName=china. Accessed 31 January 2020.

Douglas, Kate, and Anna Poletti. 2016. *Life Narratives and Youth Culture: Representation, Agency and Participation*. London: Palgrave Macmillan.

Forbes (@Forbes). 2018. .@HyeonseoLeeNK doesn't believe the North Korean regime will give up its nuclear weapons… "but I hope I'm wrong." #ForbesWomen. *Twitter*, 19 June. Accessed 24 March 2019.

Gilmore, Leigh. 2017a. *Tainted Witness: Why We Doubt What Women Say About Their Lives*. New York: Columbia University Press.

———. 2017b. Testimony. *a/b: Auto/Biography Studies* 32 (2): 307–309.

Keen, Suzanne. 2015. *Narrative Form: Revised and Expanded*, 2nd ed. Houndsmills: Palgrave Macmillan.

Keen, Suzanne. 2016. Life Writing and the Empathetic Circle. *Concentric: Literary and Cultural Studies* 42 (2): 9–26.

Kim, Jack, and Louis Charbonneau. 2013. North Korea Threatens Nuclear Strike, U.N. Expands Sanctions. *Reuters*, 7 March. https://www.reuters.com/article/us-korea-north-attack/north-korea-threatens-nuclear-strike-u-n-expands-sanctions-idUSBRE9260BR20130307. Accessed 31 January 2020.

Kurlantzick, Joshua, and Jana Mason. 2006. North Korean Refugees: The Chinese Dimension. In *The North Korean Refugee Crisis: Human Rights and International Response*, ed. Stephen Haggard and Marcus Noland, 34–52. Washington, DC: Committee for Human Rights in North Korea. https://www.hrnk.org/uploads/pdfs/The_North_Korean_Refugee_Crisis.pdf. Accessed 26 July 2017.

Lee, Hyeonseo. 2012. Life on the Other Side. Speech. *YouTube*, 31 May. https://www.youtube.com/watch?v=O3dGj5988gM. Accessed 22 March 2019.

———. 2013. My Escape from North Korea. Speech. *TED.com*, February. https://www.ted.com/talks/hyeonseo_lee_my_escape_from_north_korea. Accessed 12 March 2020.

———. 2015a. Awakening North Korea's Valley of the Clueless. Speech. *YouTube*, 13 October. https://www.youtube.com/watch?v=KP5mzWDH4b8. Accessed 22 March 2019.

———. 2015b. Why I Escaped from My Brainwashed Country. Speech. *YouTube*, 21 December. https://www.youtube.com/watch?v=Ed4SeoQypy0. Accessed 22 March 2019.

———. 2018a. @HyeonseoLeeNK. *Twitter*. https://twitter.com/hyeonseoleenk. Accessed 21 March 2019.

———. 2018b. Defector supports Trump policy in North Korea. Channel 4 News. Interview with Cathy Newman. *YouTube*, 11 March. https://www.youtube.com/watch?v=vIjNv6tnibw. Accessed 21 March 2019.

———. 2018c. Creating a United, and Welcoming, Korea. Opinion. *The New York Times*, 3 December. https://www.nytimes.com/2018/12/03/opinion/korea-hyeonseo-lee.html. Accessed 24 March 2019.

———. 2018d. @HyeonseoLeeNK. *Facebook*. https://www.facebook.com/HyeonseoLeeNK/. Accessed 31 January 2020.

———. 2019a. About Me. *Hyeonseo Lee* personal webpage. http://www.hyeonseo-lee.com/eng/about-me_27652.shtml. Accessed 12 March 2020.

———. 2019b. Media. *Hyeonseo Lee* personal webpage. http://www.hyeonseo-lee.com/eng/media_27630.shtml. Accessed 12 March 2020.

———. 2019c. News. *Hyeonseo Lee* personal webpage. http://www.hyeonseo-lee.com/eng/news_23715.shtml. Accessed 12 March 2020.

Lee, Hyeonseo, and David John. 2015. *The Girl with Seven Names: A North Korean Defector's Story*. London: William Collins.
Martínez García, Ana Belén. 2017a. Unearthing the Past: Bringing Ideological Indoctrination to Light in North Korean Girls' Memoirs. *a/b: Auto/Biography Studies* 32 (3): 587–602.
———. 2017b. Bana Alabed: Using Twitter to Draw Attention to Human Rights Violations. *Prose Studies* 39 (2–3): 132–149.
———. 2018. TED Talks as Life Writing: Online and Offline Activism. *Life Writing* 15 (4): 487–503.
———. 2019. Denouncing Human Trafficking in China: North Korean Women's Memoirs as Evidence. *State Crime Journal* 8 (1): 59–79.
Moore-Gilbert, Bart. 2009. *Postcolonial Life-Writing: Culture, Politics and Self-Representation*. Abingdon: Routledge.
Office of the United Nations High Commissioner for Refugees (UNHCR). 2010. *Convention and Protocol Relating to the Status of Refugees*. Geneva: Office of the United Nations High Commissioner for Refugees. http://www.unhcr.org/protection/basic/3b66c2aa10/conventionprotocol-relating-status-refugees.html. Accessed 28 July 2017.
Oh, Kongdan, and Ralph C. Hassig. 2000. *North Korea: Through the Looking Glass*. Washington: Brookings.
Palkot, Greg. 2017. North Korean Defector Shares Her Story of Regime Control. Interview with Hyeonseo Lee. Fox News. *YouTube*, 3 May. https://www.youtube.com/watch?v=qx5llWp-MtM. Accessed 21 March 2019.
Papacharissi, Zizi. 2012. Without You, I'm Nothing: Performances of the Self on Twitter. *International Journal of Communication* 6: 1989–2006.
Park, Yeonmi. 2014. North Korean Defector. Speech. *YouTube*, 6 November. Accessed 24 March 2019.
———. 2015. *In Order to Live: A North Korean Girl's Journey to Freedom*. London: Penguin.
Pence, Michael R. (@V7VOA). 2018a. Mike Pence. *Twitter*, 8 February. Accessed 21 March 2019.
———. 2018b. @VP. *Twitter*, 9 February. Accessed 21 March 2019.
PSCORE. 2017. People for Successful COrean REunification. http://pscore.org/newest/en/home/. Accessed 22 January 2018.
Rak, Julie. 2013. *Boom!: Manufacturing Memoir for the Popular Market*. Waterloo, ON: Wilfrid Laurier University Press.
Schaffer, Kay, and Sidonie Smith. 2004. *Human Rights and Narrated Lives: The Ethics of Recognition*. New York: Palgrave Macmillan.
Seth, Michael J. 2010. *A Concise History of Modern Korea: From the Late Nineteenth Century to the Present*. Lanham, MD: Rowman & Littlefield.
Slote, Michael. 2007. *The Ethics of Care and Empathy*. Abingdon: Routledge.

Smith, Sidonie. 2006. Narratives and Rights: *Zlata's Diary* and the Circulation of Stories of Suffering Ethnicity. *WSQ: Women's Studies Quarterly* 34 (1–2): 133–152.

Smith, Sidonie, and Julia Watson. 2002. *Interfaces: Women, Autobiography, Image, Performance*. Ann Arbor: University of Michigan Press.

———. 2010. *Reading Autobiography: A Guide for Interpreting Life Narratives*, 2nd ed. Minneapolis: Minnesota University Press.

———. 2017. *Life Writing in the Long Run: A Smith & Watson Autobiography Studies Reader*. Ann Arbor, MI: Maize Books.

Trump, Donald. 2018. @realDonaldTrump. *Twitter*, 8 February. Accessed 21 March 2019.

United Nations Security Council (UNSC). 2013. Resolution 2087. *Security Council Report*, 22 January. https://www.securitycouncilreport.org/atf/cf/%7B65BFCF9B-6D27-4E9C-8CD3-CF6E4FF96FF9%7D/s_res_2087.pdf. Accessed 31 January 2020.

UN Commission of Inquiry (COI) on Human Rights in the Democratic People's Republic of Korea. 2014a. Report of the Commission of Inquiry on Human Rights in the Democratic People's Republic of Korea. UN Doc. A/HRC/25/63, 7 February. United Nations General Assembly, Human Rights Council. https://undocs.org/A/HRC/25/63. Accessed 6 November 2017.

———. 2014b. Report of the Detailed Findings of the Commission of Inquiry on Human Rights in the Democratic People's Republic of Korea. UN Doc. A/HRC/25/CRP.1, 7 February. United Nations General Assembly, Human Rights Council. http://www.ohchr.org/EN/HRBodies/HRC/CoIDPRK/Pages/CommissionInquiryonHRinDPRK.aspx. Accessed 6 November 2017.

Watson, Julia. 2016. Parsua Bashi's *Nylon Road*: The Visual Dialogics of Witnessing in Iranian Women's Graphic Memoir. In *Life Writing in the Long Run: A Smith & Watson Autobiography Studies Reader*, ed. S. Smith and J. Watson, 679–730. Ann Arbor, MI: Maize Books.

White House. 2018a. President Trump Meets with North Korean Defectors. *YouTube*, 2 February. https://www.youtube.com/watch?v=MWL_9XmNRv4. Accessed 21 March 2019.

———. 2018b. Joint Statement of President Donald J. Trump of the United States of America and Chairman Kim Jong Un of the Democratic People's Republic of Korea at the Singapore Summit. *The White House*, 12 June. https://www.whitehouse.gov/briefings-statements/joint-statement-president-donald-j-trump-united-states-america-chairman-kim-jong-un-democratic-peoples-republic-korea-singapore-summit/. Accessed 31 January 2020.

Whitlock, Gillian. 2007. *Soft Weapons: Autobiography in Transit*. Chicago: University of Chicago Press.

———. 2015. *Postcolonial Life Narratives: Testimonial Transactions*. Oxford: Oxford University Press.

Wilson, Richard Ashby, and Richard D. Brown (eds.). 2009. *Humanitarianism and Suffering: The Mobilization of Empathy*. New York: Cambridge University Press.

CHAPTER 4

Yeonmi Park: North Korean Activist and Instagram Celebrity

Abstract This chapter is a companion to the previous one, since Lee and Park come from the very same village in North Korea and their life-writing projects capitalize on the notion of a North Korean girl who escapes, travels to China and onto a Global North final destination. Girlhood is maximized by both, but their self-narration differs in other ways. Though Park fits the girl trope of humanitarian discourse, she strives to move past the category of victim and redefine herself as a survivor. The remediation/curation of Park's self on social media platforms—but also offline—is assessed to gauge the impact those may have had in crafting a public persona, a celebrity activist, as she has been enrolled in causes beyond Korean activism, namely feminism.

Keywords Yeonmi Park · North Korea · Girlhood · Social media · Celebrity activist · Feminism

This chapter is a companion to the previous one (Chapter 3), since both Lee and Park come from the very same village in North Korea, Hyesan, and both their life-writing projects capitalize on the notion of the "North Korean girl" who manages to escape the country and her journey into China and onto a Global North final destination.[1] However, age plays an important role as the circumstances surrounding their birth vary significantly (Martínez García 2018). Thus, Hyeonseo Lee, as we

A. B. Martínez García, *New Forms of Self-Narration*, Palgrave Studies in Life Writing, https://doi.org/10.1007/978-3-030-46420-2_4

saw in the previous chapter, was born in 1980, while Yeonmi Park, the focus of the present chapter, was born in 1993. Over a decade separates their birth, which means that, "social circumstances aside, the experience of the North Korean Great Famine in the 1990s hit them at different stages of their lives" (491). Lee was already in her teens by the time she experienced hardship, whereas Park was born in its midst. Experiencing starvation in the first person shapes the narrative of Park's childhood, with hunger a repeated topic until her escape from North Korea. Some episodes include her eking out a living in the streets, the trauma of losing both status and home salient themes in her memoir. The age of these two North Korean young women activists must therefore be considered "a factor … which affects their self-presentation in noticeable ways" (491). Girlhood is maximized in both cases, but their life writing differs, as I demonstrate here, in multiple other ways.[2]

Constructing the Girl of Humanitarian Discourse

Though her geographical background may be similar to Lee's, Park has capitalized on many other factors to be as famous as she is. To begin with, through the lens of gender and age, Park fits the profile of the girl in need of help of humanitarianism (Wilson and Brown 2009), but she strives to move past the category of victim and redefine herself as a survivor.

Of all the human rights at stake in Park's testimony, of uppermost importance is the right over one's body (Martínez García 2019). A compelling image of human trafficking emerges in Yeonmi Park's (2015) memoir, *In Order to Live*, which describes events that happened when she was between 13 and 15 years old. Crucially, the most terrible things that human trafficking implies, such as rape, sexual slavery, and losing your rights over your body, are not merely witnessed but suffered by the author/narrator. Park's descriptions of the atrocities she endured illustrate what Sidonie Smith and Julia Watson mention as common uses of life writing in the context of human rights campaigns, confronting readers with "emotional, often overwhelming, accounts of dehumanization, brutal and violent physical harm, and exploitation" (Smith and Watson 2010, 133). Not taken to be a child anymore once she crosses into China at 13, in direct contradiction to Article 3(d) of the Trafficking Protocol which states that "'Child' shall mean any person under eighteen years of age" (OHCHR 2000), this first-person victimization is made even more urgent given her age, and serves the purpose of advocating for justice and redress. Invoking the testimonial power of a narrator's voice in the form of a child, particularly a girl, to express violence exerted upon them, is a trope arguably indebted to Anne Frank (Douglas and Poletti 2016, 20–22; Smith 2006, 152). The emotions excited by Park's narrative are maximized by stressing the "I" of a child witness: "The eyewitness holds a special status in narrative accounts. The attestation 'I was there' makes a unique bid for readers' attention and empathy" (Watson 2016, 683). The testimonial power of "eye-witnessing" or "I-witnessing" creates deep affective ties between reader and narrator.

Park's narrative of the traumatic events of her mother's rape (Park 2015, 125, 130) serves an advocacy agenda, denouncing the rape and trafficking suffered precisely at the hands of those who, given their common ancestry, should have helped them. One is reminded of studies that show the involvement of Korean-Chinese ethnic population in the border regions in these trafficking networks (CHRNK 2009, 17–19). That brokers and victims share Korean ancestry is particularly traumatic for the latter, mostly given the Confucianism embedded in North Korean culture with its emphasis on family and elders as figures deserving of respect as well as loving, wise, and protective (Seth 2010, 137). This ideal is shattered when these men traffic North Korean women and girls. Park's narrative is an attempt to come to terms with what she felt, a form of self-healing through writing which Suzette Henke (1998) calls "scriptotherapy" (xii), aimed at healing oneself through reliving the traumatic experience in written form and making it public. Only then, according to Dori Laub (1995), may one repossess one's life story (74). In fact, the aim of using life writing is stated by Park (2015) in her prologue, where she acknowledges her past silence regarding this issue but accepts the need to finally come forward: "the only way we can survive our own memories is to shape them into a story that makes sense out of events that seem inexplicable" (5). This matches Henke's (1998) theory that "What cannot be uttered might at least be written" (xix). Exposing the crimes committed against them, activist narrators become agents in and of their life story, while healing the wounds that trauma may have caused.

The way in which North Korean women and girls are tricked into agreeing to being sold is explained by Park (2015) as part of a process by which the brokers make them feel as if they were not human beings, which calls to mind the Universal Declaration of Human Rights (UDHR) and how these networks dehumanize people to make a profit: "'sold'? I could not imagine how one human could sell another. I thought people could sell only dogs, chickens, or other animals–not people" (Park 2015, 127).[3] Witnessing the brokers negotiating prices "right in front of us" (128) imbued Park with a deeper sense of shame:

> I will never forget the burning humiliation of listening to these negotiations, of being *turned into a piece of merchandise* in the space of a few hours. It was a feeling beyond anger. It's still hard to fathom why we went along with all of this, except that we were caught between fear and hope. We were numb … (129; emphasis added)

Once their bodies are treated as commodities and objects to trade with, their humanity fades; feelings would just be a hindrance to their survival: "our purpose was reduced to our immediate needs" (129). In fact, one of the typical symptoms associated with post-traumatic stress disorder (PTSD) is "Diminished responsiveness to the external world, referred to as 'psychic numbing' or 'emotional anesthesia'" (American Psychiatric Association [APA] 1994, 424–425).[4]

It is the aim of this chapter to identify the complex ways in which the narrating "I" is built little by little adding details that construct a self in the making. Since its inception as a literary genre, testimony has been a controversial genre, plagued with ethical problems and the well-known dilemma between the imperative to bear witness and surviving the witnessing (Felman and Laub 1992; Jensen 2019). Testimonial accounts are prone to accusations of untruth. If one admits, however, that the "I" of testimony speaks on behalf not just of one's own experiences but of those of others in a similar situation, then it is perhaps easier to accept narratives like Park's past the premises of truth value and suggest, as Smith and Watson do (2012), reading first-person testimony for its ethical value, "one that does not rely on an overinvestment in 'authenticity'" (592). Some of the most notable criticisms raised against Park are the inconsistencies in her account, subject of scathing reviews such as in Mary Ann Jolley's (2014) "The Strange Tale of Yeonmi Park" published 10 December 2014 for *The Diplomat*. Apart from the inconsistent details in her story, academics such as Jay Song (2018) in her recent chapter "The Emergence of Five North Korean Defector-Activists in Transnational Activism" have pointed out the too emotional language Yeonmi Park deploys and her reliance on sensationalist agendas (211). I am rather inclined to agree with a middle-way approach, in line with John Cussen's (2016) review essay for *Korean Studies* which begins by mentioning the critiques against Park and other North Korean memoirists (Jolley 2014; Abt 2014; Bassett 2015; Epstein and Green 2013; Power 2014), but goes on to assert the value of such testimonial memoirs.

Pervasive Online Presence: Twitter, Facebook, YouTube, Instagram

Following in the footsteps of authors like Anne Frank or Zlata Filipović, Yeonmi Park's life-writing project constructs a self of the girl victim of human rights violations who has suffered traumatizing atrocities. What's new about Park's case, though, is how, through her strategic deployment of social media, she exemplifies how testimony can travel and compel people, inviting dialogue thanks to, among other things, the technological affordances of social media (Pinchevski 2019, 88). In this section, I look at the remediation or curation of Park's self on social media platforms to gauge the impact they may have had in creating a public persona in the past few years. Already a user of both Facebook and Twitter in South Korea at 17, Park moved to live in the United States, where she opened an Instagram account in her 20s.

Park's (2020a) Twitter account was created October 2011 (@YeonmiParkNK) but it is quite intriguing to note that it has only 20,799 followers, substantially fewer than Facebook (2020b) ones and even fewer than followers on Instagram (2020c). Why is it, if this account was created much earlier? One of the reasons might be that her aggressive tone has finally caught up with her on this platform, with many trolls and verbal attacks against her and her authenticity, perhaps diluted on platforms like Facebook and Instagram, for the intention they were set up for varies—Facebook to connect with similar-minded individuals and groups, Instagram for fashionistas' selfie self-presentation (Maguire 2018).

A notable example of Park's deployment of Twitter is to, via the technological affordance of retweeting (see Martínez García 2020), align herself with many other activists and activist groups with whom she may not be directly collaborating. However, her strategy is not always reciprocated. Thus, though she follows a vast number of nongovernmental organizations and humanitarian associations, she is rarely followed by all those.

Park also announces her public interventions via Twitter (2020a). Yet, it is the conflation of the offline and online realms that explains her pervasiveness (see Martínez García 2018, 2020). Tweeting about a forthcoming event almost always coincides with appearances in the press, traditional, mainstream media, as well as independent media, giving interviews, posting the links on YouTube, and publicizing via Facebook using similar but not quite the same terminology. That way, she populates the public sphere without it giving the impression that she is merely copy-pasting the same message over and over. She is, thus seen, quite adept at self-presentation online in a way that avoids overbearingness and boredom on readers/audiences.

Park's (2020b) Facebook page was created 28 August 2014 (@OfficialYeonmiPark) and has 112,504 followers as of 12 March 2020. Perhaps a decision was made to contribute to other debates, more specialized and academic, than approaching the general public via tweets. The tone of Park's tweets compared to that of her Facebook posts seems to back up the claim that she is likely striving to come across as more mature and professional on Facebook than on Twitter. An exception might be the addition of photographs previously uploaded on Instagram supplied with extensive textual background on Facebook, something neither Twitter nor Instagram usually do. Yet, by making users complicit in her other social media worlds, she turns their attention to one or the other, the more social or the more personal features of her life, thus ensuring maximal impact.

YouTube has played an important role in disseminating Park's video testimonials (interviews, TEDx talks, public speeches). The interplay of this platform and other social media platforms is paramount, with one medium feeding the other in an ongoing cycle that accounts for the virality of her talks and the number of followers she has on those digital platforms (see Martínez García 2020).

On 4 April 2016 Park created an Instagram account (@yeonmi_park), where she has a growing number of followers on Instagram—33,671 so far (2020c), which may grant an analysis of behavior on that platform as that of an "Instagirl" (Maguire 2018, 179) which Emma Maguire defines as "a life style blogger and social media influencer who uses her self-brand to advertise products on social media, and she is an increasingly pervasive identity in the media landscape" (184). Yeonmi Park collaborates with several brands in the process of branding herself, so she arguably fits the mold of Instagram influencer. As opposed to Facebook (2020b), where Park appears as a Coachella girl, or Twitter (2020a), where she appears as both professional speaker and ranting girl against the North Korean regime, what she does on Instagram (2020c) is clearly present herself as a fashionista. Whenever she is about to participate in a public event of any kind, she resorts to posting selfies and other photographs onto Instagram, to mark clearly where she is located or geographically tagged. That way, Park maximizes the effect of proximity to those she is about to perhaps meet out of the virtual public sphere and in the actual physical world.

As much as Park shows one different version of herself every time she gives a public presentation, she also presents herself differently depending on the platform she is deploying. That is not to say that she is a different person altogether in each of those media. However, she presents versions that may at times contradict each other (see Park 2014a, b, c, d, 2015, 2020c) but, more often than not, provide extra information that creates a richer, constructed version of this multifaceted individual (Martínez García 2018, 498).

In a similar vein to how YouTubers and "Instagirls" (Maguire 2018, 179) find fame online that may rapidly translate into their offline lives, one might say Yeonmi Park is a celebrity activist. Indeed, she has been enrolled in causes beyond the scope of Korean activism, namely feminism, featuring in Tory Burch's #EmbraceAmbition campaign (O'Connor 2017). As pointed out at the start of this section, Park has arguably become a persona, a public face easily identifiable, an icon in the media across multiple domains that may be at odds with her private life but is perpetually being updated and reconstructed (see Martínez García 2020).

Comparing Park's TEDx Talk to Lee's TED Talk[5]

Yeonmi Park's TEDx talk (2014d), "North Korean Defector," delivered at Bath in November 2014, is carefully staged to present an activist self in front of a British audience of young people with whom they can relate. In order to engender empathic identification, she must therefore be appraised as similar to them, beyond the barriers of otherness that language and culture may pose, what Julia Ludewig (2017) identifies in TED talks as "a symbolic flattening of the difference between audience and speaker" (6). This is similar to how Suzanne Keen (2016) sees strategic empathy in life writing, where "common human experiences, feelings, hopes, and vulnerabilities" (22) are stressed in order to "transcend differences" (20). Taking a closer look at the strategies she deploys to present her activist self, I first attend to the title of her talk as it appears when you Google it: "North Korean Defector." She is by no means the first defector to escape her country. Nevertheless, she appropriates that role for herself. Furthermore, those words become her presentation card, as the message is flashed on the screen right below her name. The strategic placement of those words is perceived as an intrinsic part of her identity, one and the same with her name.

A close reading of Park's text leads to perceive how she constructs her narrative in crescendo, both with regard to the emotions displayed and animated in others and the topics under discussion, moving from the personal details of her life story to an open denunciation of gross human rights violations. Park's language changes accordingly to match her switch from a personal to a political discourse, moving from the use of the pronoun "I" to the pronoun "we," involving the audience in the process: "*I* often *saw dead bodies* on the street and then when I go [sic] to school *I saw* lots of *dead bodies* and sometimes *dead bodies* floating on the river, and *I never felt* any emotion for that. That was my routine life" (2014d; emphasis added). Following Keen's (2016) theory of narrative empathy, Park is combining both "broadcast strategic empathy"—relying on universals that foster common ground (Keen 2016, 22)—with "ambassadorial strategic empathy"—insisting on the plight of a particular group of individuals far removed from the audience (20)—so as to make her message more durable than if any of the strategies were used in isolation. Park's "I" is powerful in reaching out to her audience, seeking an emotional response that she was not allowed to display at the time due to indoctrination (Martínez García 2017), as she will assert by the end of her speech. Her "I" is that of a young girl, who, on her way to school, was forced to contemplate death, a traumatic memory hard to erase. She builds her speech around her witnessing role, insisting on the fact that she "saw" what she is describing. Finally, the focus is on those "dead bodies" she saw and the numbing effect they may have had on her. By choosing to speak of those memories long repressed, she is both healing an identity at stake (Henke 1998, xii; Nelson 2001, 22) and denouncing the horrors no child should be faced with (Schultheis 2008; Emberley 2009; Wilson and Brown 2009). Park's "School recollections reveal facts hidden from public view and restore them to light" (Martínez García 2017, 598) and recreate the past as one filled with state crimes and indoctrination. In so doing, she is writing her "counter-history" (Schaffer and Smith 2004, 42), defying the sanctioned state narrative. Using her witnessing act as a first-person testimony, Park aligns herself with a long-standing tradition of authors before her.

"We," in Park's speech (2014d), does not stand for just Yeonmi and her mother, or Yeonmi and other North Koreans, but members of the audience as well, demanding active involvement (Ludewig 2017, 5; Boltanski 1999, xv). Park's emotional discourse throughout her narrative is meant to encourage a range of emotions as varied as sadness, compassion, or even anger. To strike an emotional chord in the audience, she deploys diverse emotions, shyly giggling at the beginning at the mention of playing video games, while building up tension in the awful, dramatic account of witnessing death and rape. By thus embedding the personal in the political, the private and the public are conflated, a convergence making them inextricable parts of her identity, an "inherent element" of how she lives online and off (McNeill and Zuern 2015, xii).

Much could be said about the emphatic repetition of key words throughout Park's discourse. Malala Yousafzai's (Chapter 2) famous speech at the United Nations in defense of human rights,[6] was, after all, viral at the time Park gave this talk, which may have influenced her style, notably through the inclusion of rhetorical strategies such as repetition and quotes by famous rights activists. Modeling her speech on Yousafzai's, therefore, Park finishes her intervention by adapting a civil rights catchphrase to suit her denunciation of the North Korean dictatorship: "Martin Luther King Jr said, '*injustice* anywhere is *injustice* everywhere.' Let's do what we can to eliminate the *injustice* of the Kim regime. Thank you very much" (Park 2014d; emphasis added). Her repetition of the word "injustice" at the end of her talk is strategically placed. In combination with a global icon of rights campaigns and her broad call to action ("Let's do what we can"), these last sentences are not only intentional but the key to reading the whole text. She is not an individual narrating her personal vicissitudes. Rather, she is constructing a collective identity, enacting a communal role, standing for the community of oppressed North Koreans, lending a voice to those unheard, and making ethical claims on the readers/audience of her "visual-verbal narrative" (Smith and Watson 2002, 380).

In contrast to Hyeonseo Lee's (Chapter 3) narrating "I," Yeonmi Park's narrating "I" quickly develops into a collective "we" which is full of emotional force, aimed at representing not just her story of victimization and survival but the suffering of a whole people. Importantly, Park presents herself as both a North Korean defector and part of a bigger community, namely the human family, a radical choice that brings her closer to her audience while setting her apart from Lee, who relies on a much more humanitarian reading of her text, asking outsiders in positions of power to change things for North Koreans. Those two attitudes, though blatantly dissimilar, are aimed at precisely the same objective—helping North Koreans. They present two different, intriguingly at odds but yet compatible ways of looking at North Korean people. Their discourses and life-writing texts are ultimately imbricated in those of larger organizations and thus employed to raise awareness and facilitate change. Their reliance on tropes of witnessing and innocence are highly strategic. In *Spectacular Rhetorics*, Wendy S. Hesford (2011) stresses how "the human rights spectacle is made to exert pressure on truth-telling conventions to achieve political effects and to manipulate affect" (23). Lee and Park choose to purposefully focus on their traumatic childhood in their TED talks. In so doing, they inscribe themselves in larger frameworks for social justice, calling to mind popular tropes such as the victimized child of human rights discourse (151–187). They deploy other rhetorical weapons, among them the alternation between personal and political stance noticeable in their choice of pronouns, their call for humanitarian response, or their inherent success story that sets the background for their storied performance on and offline.

Offline Life Writing: Memoir

Several narrative strategies are at play in Park's (2015) memoir. To begin with, Park's relation to empathy is very much conflicted. On the one hand, she spends much of the memoir claiming she did not feel any emotions; on the other hand, that very claim makes for a very emotional storyline. It is precisely when she discovers others who are not North Koreans suffering, that she realizes they need "compassion" (Park 2015, 250), and, by extension, so does she. This is key to the way the narrative of both this text and other life-writing texts in Park's life-writing project are shaped. They consistently advocate for the need for empathy, and they do so by exercising "authorial strategic empathy" as described by Suzanne Keen (2016). As with the other young women activists contained in this volume, Park highlights the plight of the suffering other—"ambassadorial" empathizing (Keen 2016, 20)—while also insisting on what humans share—"broadcast" empathizing (22). With both types of empathy, the narrating "I" succeeds in turning the reader into an "ethical witness" (Whitlock 2007, 77) and so potentially more prone to become active and engage in her or like-minded activism.

Calling to mind Genette's (1997) "paratexts," Park's (2015) dedication suggests a connection to "freedom" fighters (2015, v), as if in a direct bid for positioning herself within the category of social justice activist, be that for civil rights, human rights, or any other minority group who raise their voice. Her words, "for anyone, anywhere, struggling for freedom" have a universal tone, opening her plight to others beyond North Koreans whose voices may be repressed and suppressed. This seeming contradiction with what the title and the cover suggest the book will be on, namely the story of a "North Korean Girl" (Park 2015), holds the tension between the ethnic particular and the universal, which will permeate the memoir and the whole of Park's life-writing project.

Even though Yeonmi Park does not present her identity crisis as the central message of her memoir (2015) like Hyeonseo Lee does in hers (Lee and John 2015) (Chapter 3), looking closely at Park's text (2015) one can grasp the extent to which she did indeed suffer inner turmoil from a very young age. With the benefit of hindsight, Park can look back at her past and see what amounted to a numbed self who lacked the ability to care for others.

The "I" of Park's (2015) memoir does not go through so many individual transformations as the "I" of Lee's (Lee and John 2015), which boasts up to 7 name changes (see Chapter 3). Park's "I" is, though, an "I" that evolves in time: a sheltered "I" protected by her family—"there was human intimacy and connection, something that is hard to find in the modern world I inhabit today" (2015, 13), a robotic "we"—"We have to do everything at the same time, always. So at noon, when the radio goes '*beeep*,' everybody stops to eat lunch. There is no getting away from it" (67), a ravenous "I"—"All I wanted was to have something to eat for my next meal … with an animal instinct to survive, unconsciously calculating how much longer each bite of food will keep your body going" (104), a numbed "I"—"I felt dead inside, and perhaps I was" (170), a South Korean "I"—"I was determined to lose the one thing that gave away my identity as a defector, so when I talked to people I practiced speaking in a South Korean accent" (226), the "I" of a "privileged North Korean" who was called the "Paris Hilton of North Korea" by television producers (243), an "I" in crisis—"I still wasn't sure who I was myself or who I wanted to be" (245), a North Korean activist "I"—"defectors with English skills were needed to give a voice to the millions of North Koreans behind a wall of silence and oppression … I wasn't sure what a human rights activist was. Now suddenly people were telling me I was becoming the face of this issue" (258–259). The tension between an individual and a collective consciousness is also part of the identity crisis she endures, one that owes much of the (physical and psychological) hardship to the brainwashing education she received (see Martínez García 2017).

A brief note must be made on the editorial choice to leave out Park's co-author, Maryanne Vollers, famous ghostwriter and journalist, from the copyright agreement, effacing the official narrative of subjugated other and empowering Park's voice as authenticated author. Among Vollers's ghostwritten memoirs, which she calls "collaborations" on her personal website (Vollers 2019), feature some important titles on relevant female leaders and public figures in the United States, such as international bestseller Hillary Clinton's *Living History* (Clinton 2003) on the struggles of becoming a female politician; Ashley Judd's *All That Is Bitter & Sweet* (Judd and Vollers 2011), another bestseller, this time on Judd's humanitarian enterprises; Jerry Nielsen's *Ice Bound* (Nielsen and Vollers 2001), #1 New York Times Bestseller on survival against the odds and human resilience; and Sissy Spacek's *My Extraordinary Ordinary Life* (Spacek and Vollers 2012), on women's coming of age and self-empowerment. Throughout these titles, one gets a sense of a narrative thread intent on exploring women's difficulties in leading their lives in the public eye, always scrutinized and pressurized. Their stories rely on the tropes of the girl in need, the woman coming of age and a rags-to-riches storyline. Common to all these memoirs is the happy ending, emphasizing success and the resilience that was needed to get to that point. They all serve to validate a feminist narrative and, therefore, a feminist activism agenda.

Park's literary agent is, curiously, the same as Malala Yousafzai's (Chapter 2), Karolina Sutton, at Curtis Brown. Besides, Park's (2015) memoir was published by Penguin Fig Tree, an imprint of Penguin Random House. The fact that such an important publisher as Penguin backs the publication of Park's (2015) memoir is vital if one is to explain its wide distribution and best-selling numbers.

The Oddity of Park's YouTube Channel

As a bit of a curiosity, this final part in the chapter is devoted to Park's (2019) short-lived experiment in life-writing online—a YouTube channel she created on 11 June 2018 to livestream comment on the Trump-Kim historical summit. Only days later, on 23 June 2018, she uploaded her most famous public speech from back in 2014 at the Oslo Freedom

Forum and nothing else has been uploaded as of March 2020. A possible explanation for why she has not continued to add to the channel could well be the little change in US-DPRK relations since then. This might also be coupled with the fact that she is living in New York City, in the United States, so it would not be very wise to criticize the government as outspokenly as she was doing. Perhaps lack of support for her particular take on the summit, as shown in the quite small number of subscriptions for this channel—5120 as of 12 March 2020, also made an impact on her decision to discontinue this approach, favoring platforms such as Instagram instead, a radical departure from this original experiment in life writing.

Notes

1. In a similar way, Chapters 5 and 6 in this volume look at how two young women activists—Bana Alabed and Nujeen Mustafa—seemingly compete for the title of "Syrian girl."
2. This chapter is derived in part from an article published in *a/b: Auto/Biography Studies* (2017) © The Autobiography Society, available online: https://www.tandfonline.com/doi/abs/10.1080/08989575.2017.1338004; an article published in *Life Writing* (2018) © Taylor & Francis, available online: https://www.tandfonline.com/doi/full/10.1080/14484528.2017.1405317; and an article published in *State Crime Journal* (2019) © Pluto Journals, available online: https://www.jstor.org/stable/10.13169/statecrime.8.1.0059.
3. Article 3(b) of the Trafficking Protocol asserts that, no matter the trafficked person's consent, vulnerable subjects should be protected (OHCHR 2000). Such position of vulnerability leading girls and women into forced marriage further contravenes Article 16(b) of the Convention on the Elimination of All Forms of Discrimination against Women (OHCHR 1979) to which China is also a State party, as well as Article 23(3) of the International Covenant on Civil and Political Rights by which "No marriage shall be entered into without the free and full consent of the intending spouses" (OHCHR 1966).
4. Previous studies suggest North Korean refugees experience symptoms akin to PTSD (Haggard and Nolan 2011, 36–41), both when interviewed in South Korea (Baubet et al. 2003; Jeon 2000; Jeon et al. 2005) and in China (Lee et al. 2001; Chang et al. 2006, 14–33). See Chapter 7 in this volume for a similar narrative of sexual slavery, commoditization, and trauma from a different geographical background—Nadia Murad's testimonial life-writing project as an example of self-reconstruction against ISIS control over Yazidi girls and women in Iraq.

5. This section was originally published in an article "TED Talks as Life Writing: Online and Offline Activism" in the journal *Life Writing* (Martínez García 2018, 494–497) © Taylor & Francis, available online: https://www.tandfonline.com/doi/full/10.1080/14484528.2017.1405317.
6. See Chapter 2.

Works Cited

Abt, Felix. 2014. Dead Bodies Are Piling Up Rotting on North Korea's Streets and Floating in Its Rivers. Blog post. *Goodreads*, 20 October. https://www.goodreads.com/author_blog_posts/8090657-dead-bodies-are-piling-up-rotting-on-north-korea-s-streets-and. Accessed 3 April 2019.

American Psychiatric Association (APA). 1994. *Diagnostic and Statistical Manual of Mental Health Disorders*, 4th ed. Washington, DC: American Psychiatric Association.

Bassett, Michael. 2015. Modern Warfare Korea: The Weaponization of Human Rights. *Counterpunch*, 11 September. https://www.counterpunch.org/2015/09/11/modern-warfare-korea-the-weaponization-of-human-rights/. Accessed 3 April 2019.

Baubet, Thierry, Marine Buissonnière, Sophie Delaunay, and Pierre Salignon. 2003. Réfugiés nord-coréens en Corée du Sud. De l'importance d'un tiers humanitaire [North Korean Refugees in South Korea: The Importance of a Humanitarian Third Party]. *L'Autre* 3 (4): 455–469.

Boltanski, Luc. 1999. *Distant Suffering: Morality, Media and Politics*, trans. G. Burchell. Cambridge: Cambridge University Press.

Chang, Yoonok, Stephan Haggard, and Marcus Noland. 2006. North Korean Refugees in China: Evidence from a Survey. In *The North Korean Refugee Crisis: Human Rights and International Response*, ed. S. Haggard and M. Noland, 14–33. Washington, DC: US Committee for Human Rights in North Korea. https://www.hrnk.org/uploads/pdfs/The_North_Korean_Refugee_Crisis.pdf. Accessed 30 July 2017.

Clinton, Hillary Rodham. 2003. *Living History*. New York: Simon & Schuster.

Committee for Human Rights in North Korea (CHRNK). 2009. *Lives for Sale: Personal Accounts of Women Fleeing North Korea to China*. Washington, DC: Committee for Human Rights in North Korea. https://www.hrnk.org/uploads/pdfs/Lives_for_Sale.pdf. Accessed 6 February 2020.

Cussen, John. 2016. On the Call to Dismiss North Korean Defectors' Memoirs and on Their Dark American Alternative. *Korean Studies* 40: 140–158.

Douglas, Kate, and Anna Poletti. 2016. *Life Narratives and Youth Culture: Representation, Agency and Participation*. London: Palgrave Macmillan.

Emberley, Julia. 2009. A Child Is Testifying: Testimony and the Cultural Construction of Childhood in a Trans/National Frame. *Journal of Postcolonial Writing* 45 (4): 378–388.

Epstein, Stephen, and Christopher Green. 2013. Now on My Way to Meet Who? South Korean Television, North Korean Refugees, and the Dilemmas of Representation. *The Asia-Pacific Journal* 11 (41.2): 1–19. https://apjjf.org/-Christopher-Green–Stephen-Epstein/4007/article.pdf. Accessed 3 April 2019.

Felman, Shoshana, and Dori Laub. 1992. *Testimony: Crises of Witnessing in Literature, Psychoanalysis and History*. New York: Routledge.

Genette, Gérard. 1997. *Paratexts: Thresholds of Interpretation*, trans. Jane E. Lewin. Cambridge: Cambridge University Press.

Haggard, Stephan, and Marcus Nolan. 2011. *Witness to Transformation: Refugee Insights into North Korea*. Washington, DC: Peter G. Peterson Institute for International Economics.

Henke, Suzette A. 1998. *Shattered Subjects: Trauma and Testimony in Women's Life-Writing*. New York: St. Martin's Press.

Hesford, Wendy S. 2011. *Spectacular Rhetorics: Human Rights Visions, Recognitions, Feminisms*. Durham: Duke University Press.

Jensen, Meg. 2019. *The Art and Science of Trauma and the Autobiographical: Negotiated Truths*. Cham: Palgrave Macmillan.

Jeon, Woo Taek. 2000. Issues and Problems in Adaptation of North Korean Defectors to South Korean Society: An In-Depth Interview Study with 32 Defectors. *Yonsei Medical Journal* 41 (3): 362–371.

Jeon, WooTaek, ChangHyung Hong, ChangHo Lee, Dong Kee Kim, Mooyoung Han, and SungKil Min. 2005. Correlation Between Traumatic Events and Posttraumatic Stress Disorder Among North Korean Defectors in South Korea. *Journal of Traumatic Stress* 18 (2): 147–154.

Jolley, Mary Ann. 2014. The Strange Tale of Yeonmi Park. *The Diplomat*, 10 December. https://thediplomat.com/2014/12/the-strange-tale-of-yeonmi-park/. Accessed 29 March 2019.

Judd, Ashley, and Maryanne Vollers. 2011. *All That Is Bitter & Sweet: A Memoir*. New York: Ballantine Books.

Keen, Suzanne. 2016. Life Writing and the Empathetic Circle. *Concentric: Literary and Cultural Studies* 42 (2): 9–26.

Laub, Dori. 1995. Truth and Testimony: The Process and the Struggle. In *Trauma: Explorations in Memory*, ed. Cathy Caruth, 61–75. Baltimore: Johns Hopkins University Press.

Lee, Hyeonseo, and David John. 2015. *The Girl with Seven Names: A North Korean Defector's Story*. London: William Collins.

Lee, Yunhwan, Myung Ken Lee, Ki Hong Chun, Yeon Kyung Lee, and Soo Jin Yoon. 2001. Trauma Experience of North Korean Refugees in China. *American Journal of Preventative Medicine* 20 (3): 225–229.

Ludewig, Julia. 2017. TED Talks as an Emergent Genre. *CLCWeb: Comparative Literature and Culture* 19 (1). https://doi.org/10.7771/1481-4374.2946.

Maguire, Emma. 2018. *Girls, Autobiography, Media: Gender and Self-Mediation in Digital Economies*. Cham: Palgrave Macmillan.

Martínez García, Ana Belén. 2017. Unearthing the Past: Bringing Ideological Indoctrination to Light in North Korean Girls' Memoirs. *a/b: Auto/Biography Studies* 32 (3): 587–602.

———. 2018. TED Talks as Life Writing: Online and Offline Activism. *Life Writing* 15 (4): 487–503.

———. 2019. Denouncing Human Trafficking in China: North Korean Women's Memoirs as Evidence. *State Crime Journal* 8 (1): 59–79.

———. 2020. Women Activists' Strategies of Online Self-Presentation. *AI & Society: Journal of Knowledge, Culture and Communication*: Special Issue on Iteration as Persuasion in a Digital World. Forthcoming.

McNeill, Laurie, and John David Zuern. 2015. Online Lives 2.0: Introduction. *Biography* 38 (2): v–xlvi.

Nelson, Hilde Lindemann. 2001. *Damaged Identities: Narrative Repair*. Ithaca: Cornell University Press.

Nielsen, Jerry, and Maryanne Vollers. 2001. *Ice Bound: A Doctor's Incredible Battle for Survival at the South Pole*. New York: Talk Miramax Books.

O'Connor, Clare. 2017. Fashion Mogul Tory Burch Talks Ambitious Women and Equal Pay. *Forbes*, 8 March. Accessed 18 January 2019.

Office of the United Nations High Commissioner for Human Rights (OHCHR). 1966. International Covenant on Civil and Political Rights. United Nations General Assembly. No. 14668, 19 December. https://treaties.un.org/doc/publication/unts/volume%20999/volume-999-i-14668-english.pdf. Accessed 6 November 2017.

———. 1979. Convention on the Elimination of All Forms of Discrimination Against Women. http://www.ohchr.org/Documents/ProfessionalInterest/cedaw.pdf. Accessed 5 December 2017.

———. 2000. Protocol to Prevent, Suppress and Punish Trafficking in Persons. https://www.ohchr.org/en/professionalinterest/pages/protocoltraffickinginpersons.aspx. Accessed 30 July 2017.

Park, Yeonmi. 2014a. I Am a North Korean Millennial. Liberty in North Korea. *YouTube*, 11 July. https://www.youtube.com/watch?v=uDXkdjx7VAE&t=2s. Accessed 5 February 2020.

———. 2014b. Escaping from North Korea in Search of Freedom. One Young World. *YouTube*, 18 October. https://www.youtube.com/watch?v=ufhKWfPSQOw&t=53s. Accessed 5 February 2020.

———. 2014c. North Korea's Black Market Generation. Oslo Freedom Forum. *YouTube*, 29 October. https://www.youtube.com/watch?v=UyWsJ6NFMpE&t=4s. Accessed 5 February 2020.

———. 2014d. North Korean Defector. TEDxYouth@Bath. *YouTube*, 6 November. https://www.youtube.com/watch?v=Sg3kC4uKDJU&t=4s. Accessed 5 February 2020.

———. 2015. *In Order to Live: A North Korean Girl's Journey to Freedom*. London: Penguin.

———. 2019. Yeonmi Park. YouTube channel. *YouTube*. https://www.youtube.com/channel/UCpQu57KgT7gOoLCAu3FFQsA/featured. Accessed 12 March 2020.

———. 2020a. @YeonmiParkNK. *Twitter*. https://twitter.com/yeonmiparknk. Accessed 12 March 2020.

———. 2020b. @OfficialYeonmiPark. *Facebook*. https://www.facebook.com/OfficialYeonmiPark/. Accessed 12 March 2020.

———. 2020c. @yeonmi_park. *Instagram*. https://www.instagram.com/yeonmi_park/. Accessed 12 March 2020.

Pinchevski, Amit. 2019. *Transferred Wounds: Media and the Mediation of Trauma*. New York: Oxford University Press.

Power, John. 2014. North Korea: Defectors and Their Skeptics. *The Diplomat*, 29 October. https://thediplomat.com/2014/10/north-korea-defectors-and-their-skeptics/. Accessed 5 February 2020.

Schaffer, Kay, and Sidonie Smith. 2004. *Human Rights and Narrated Lives: The Ethics of Recognition*. New York: Palgrave Macmillan.

Schultheis, Alexandra. 2008. African Child Soldiers and Humanitarian Consumption. *Peace Review* 20 (1): 31–40.

Seth, Michael J. 2010. *A Concise History of Modern Korea: From the Late Nineteenth Century to the Present*. Lanham, MD: Rowman & Littlefield.

Smith, Sidonie. 2006. Narratives and Rights: *Zlata's Diary* and the Circulation of Stories of Suffering Ethnicity. *WSQ: Women's Studies Quarterly* 34 (1–2): 133–152.

Smith, Sidonie, and Julia Watson. 2002. *Interfaces: Women, Autobiography, Image, Performance*. Ann Arbor: University of Michigan Press.

———. 2010. *Reading Autobiography: A Guide for Interpreting Life Narratives*, 2nd ed. Minneapolis: Minnesota University Press.

———. 2012. Witness or False Witness?: Metrics of Authenticity, Collective I-Formations, and the Ethic of Verification in First-Person Testimony. *Biography* 35 (4): 590–626.

Song, Jay. 2018. The Emergence of Five North Korean Defector-Activists in Transnational Activism. In *North Korean Human Rights: Activists and Networks*, ed. A. Yeo and D. Chubb, 201–223. Cambridge: Cambridge University Press.

Spacek, Sissy, and Maryanne Vollers. 2012. *My Extraordinary Ordinary Life*. New York: Hyperion.

Vollers, Maryanne. 2019. Books. Personal website. http://www.maryannevollers.com/books.html. Accessed 12 March 2020.

Watson, Julia. 2016. Parsua Bashi's *Nylon Road*: The Visual Dialogics of Witnessing in Iranian Women's Graphic Memoir. In *Life Writing in the Long Run: A Smith & Watson Autobiography Studies Reader*, ed. S. Smith and J. Watson, 679–730. Ann Arbor, MI: Maize Books.

Whitlock, Gillian. 2007. *Soft Weapons: Autobiography in Transit*. Chicago: University of Chicago Press.

Wilson, Richard Ashby, and Richard D. Brown (eds.). 2009. *Humanitarianism and Suffering: The Mobilization of Empathy*. Cambridge: Cambridge University Press.

CHAPTER 5

Bana Alabed: From Twitter War Child to Peace Icon

Abstract This chapter examines Bana Alabed's harnessing Twitter to construct an activist self. It analyzes the intriguing ways technological and affective affordances made it possible for a 7-year-old Syrian girl to report from a war zone. Alabed has evolved past the trope of innocent suffering child typical of human rights narratives, and on to a discourse of peace and fraternity which has awarded her several prizes. Mediation—and the role her mother has played—as well as imagery to convey trauma should be further addressed and problematized. The chapter closes with a reflection on names. Like Malala, Bana is mainly known by just her first name. Getting to know these girls on a first-name basis is crucial for the degree of empathizing that may be reached.

Keywords Bana Alabed · Twitter · Technological and affective affordances · Mediation · First name · Empathizing

Bana Alabed is a Syrian girl who, aged seven, became famous overnight because of the tweets she started posting from besieged Aleppo at the height of the conflict. Thanks to her mother's help and mediation, Bana's short audiovisual and written messages were mostly carried out in English. In them, she criticized the inaction of the international community as well as the bombs coming from Russia and Syria. Though criticized for being used, biased, or a hoax, she managed to be taken out of the country

A. B. Martínez García, *New Forms of Self-Narration*, Palgrave Studies in Life Writing, https://doi.org/10.1007/978-3-030-46420-2_5

together with her family by Turkey, where they have been granted citizenship. She is heralded as a global peace icon, receiving several awards, even as she continues to resort to quite virulent attacks on the aforementioned topics.

Harnessing Twitter to Construct an Activist Self[1]

This chapter examines Bana Alabed's harnessing Twitter to construct an activist self to "show how the emotional investment triggered by first-person child narration is central to processes of social advocacy, and how the visual impact of still and moving images has the power to move audiences worldwide at a very rapid pace thanks to the digital paradigm" (Martínez García 2017b, 134). First, I analyze the intriguing ways "technological and affective affordances" (145) have made it possible for this (then) 7-year-old Syrian girl to report from a war zone, in fact enabling the youngest-ever life writer from a conflict zone to speak out about her daily life and the dangers and suffering it entailed. Back in September 2016, when Bana Alabed starting tweeting from besieged Aleppo, a Syrian city epitomizing the height of the conflict at the time, her name came to be synonymous with the Syrian war: "Her emotional texts, photos, and videos made her an internet sensation" earning her hundreds of thousands of followers on Twitter and the attention of international news media channels (132).

Assuming the answer to Kylie Cardell's (2014) question, "Can serial autobiographical posts on Twitter come to constitute a diary narrative of some sort?" (4) to be positive while moving diaries from the private to the public sphere, the focus of life writing in war zones is of political consequence (86). Bana Alabed's "auto/tweetography" (McNeill 2014) is modeled on that of another young woman who endured wartime, namely Anne Frank (Martínez García 2017b, 135). In choosing that particular template, she exemplifies a trend for young women life writers, examples of which may be Zlata Filipović in Sarajevo (Smith 2006), Farah Baker in Palestine (Wolf 2015), Malala Yousafzai in Pakistan (Martínez García 2019a; see also Chapter 2), North Korean activists like Hyeonseo Lee and Yeonmi Park (Martínez García 2017a, 2018, 2019b; see also Chapters 3 and 4), and various other youth (Douglas 2010, 2018; Douglas and Poletti 2016). This formula has been called "the Anne Frank phenomenon" (Gregoire 2016) or Anne Frank's "afterlives" (Horowitz 2012). The media have exploited this link, with *The Washington Post* going as far as to name Bana Alabed "our era's Anne Frank" (Gibson 2016). Meanwhile, others remain wary of the consequences of such reductionism (Prose 2015).

Indeed, Bana Alabed's testimony was not the first to emerge from Syria. Others before her had turned to the digital paradigm to document their lives and the ongoing abuses. Most, however, fall under the category of citizen journalists as they tend to be adult bloggers, more experienced in both writing and technology. In this regard, though blogs played a vital role in shaping people's awareness and public opinion (Göksun 2015, 20), they did not gain the emotional impact that a child's life-writing project on Twitter, an "always-on" platform (Papacharissi 2012, 2000), would have: "Radically different because written by a child, even if helped by her mother to write and speak in English, Bana Alabed's Twitter account is more emotional than factual, presenting the reader/viewer with problematic ethical choices, asking for witnesses to a child's plight" (Martínez García 2017b, 137). Considering the reliance of human rights life writing on the trope of the universal suffering child Kate Douglas and Anna Poletti (2016) suggest children and youth can actually reclaim agency by enacting that very role (68–70). This is of special significance in the case of ethnic childhood narrating themselves while incorporating tropes, genres, and strategies typical from Western discourse (Moore-Gilbert 2009). For better or worse, "The image of the child is deployed strategically as a means to a political end" (Martínez García 2017b, 137–138).[2] Age, gender, and beauty, three characteristics that seemingly link up the chapters in this book, make for the "archetypical suffering child" (Martínez García 2019a, 210) of humanitarian campaigns,[3] "at the expense of many more stories that have been silenced in the process of transforming her into a celebrity" (Martínez García 2017b, 138).

From her first tweets, Bana Alabed has been identified as "the Aleppo girl" thanks, to a large extent, to a specific technological affordance of Twitter—tagging: "tagging both categorizes the performance and makes it accessible to wider audiences. It thus affords performative statements of the self greater visibility, effectively eponymizing them" (Papacharissi 2012, 2000). The hashtag #Aleppo made her famous overnight, being endorsed by users and quickly becoming a trending topic. An example of her tweets might be: "I am very afraid I will die tonight. This [sic] bombs will kill me now. – Bana #Aleppo" (@AlabedBana, 10:00—2 Oct. 2016). The tweet features Bana Alabed holding her fingers in her ears so as to muffle the noise of bombs falling around her. Her "I" here, much as other girl activists, "represents a community of oppressed others" (Martínez García 2017a, 599). But Bana's signature together with the hashtag highlights a joint identity, a self that is constructed as a girl's first name and a tagged place, and so is very much individual but also collective. None of the two identities would exist in isolation, but from then on Bana becomes well known by just her first name, as well as others calling her a girl tweeting from Aleppo, with both competing discourses leading to one and the same life-writing activist.

Once in Turkey, Bana's tweets have been periodically switching from the carefree life of a schoolgirl to irate remarks on sustained crimes in Syria. In the latter, politicians are publicly addressed and called to account for the human rights transgressions taking place on Syrian soil and their inaction. Among the world leaders she has addressed is US President Donald Trump. On the eve of his inauguration, Bana posted an open letter where she suggested the welfare of Syrian children was in his hands:

> I know you will be the president of America so can you please *save* the children and people of Syria?
>
> You must *do something* for the children of Syria because they are like your children and deserve peace like you. If you promise me you will *do something* for the children of Syria I am already your new friend. (@AlabedBana, 9:26—25 January 2017; emphasis added)

Appealing to the United States as capable of saving lives across the planet, Bana's discourse is heavily invested in the ethics of humanitarianism. After Trump did drop some bombs on the Syrian arsenal of chemical weapons, Bana expressed open support: "I am a Syrian child who suffered under Bashar al Assad Putin. I *welcome* Donald Trump [sic] *action against the killers of my people*" (@AlabedBana, 0:42—7 Apr. 2017; emphasis added), which led to harsh criticism in the form of Twitter replies accusing her, for example, of being "pretty hypocritical" for suddenly supporting violence instead of peace (@pinningjenny, 7 Apr. 2017), others doubting whether her account was being used by "ISIS" (@Xerxesss, 7 Apr. 2017), by other "rebels" (@gomgoor, 7 Apr. 2017), or was "fake" (@garethicke, 8 Apr. 2017).

Bana's rhetoric is aggressive, which is perhaps more impactful as it is unexpectedly coming from a girl. The "narrative structures of Twitter lend form to affective modalities of storytelling" (Papacharissi 2015, 12). The affordances of Twitter, such as the 140-character limit,[4] which "specifically enables condensed performances of the self" (2012, 1990), help amplify those short messages further. Bana's tweets continue to alternate between raging rants and harrowing visuals and on to a smiling happy childhood. Yet, it is this latter discourse of peace and fraternity that has captured prize-worthy recognition.

Tweeting as a Peace Icon

How can we account for the fact that, now aged 10, Bana's tweets sometimes seem to be more simple than the ones written from Aleppo aged 7? Mediation is no doubt an issue that needs to be further addressed and problematized. The role that her mother has played in shaping Bana's life writing is central and one must assume the narrating "I" is therefore not just Bana's but a "co-constructed 'I'" (Martínez García 2017b, 143), as acknowledged on her Twitter profile (@AlabedBana). In what follows, I take a closer look at Bana Alabed's tweets ever since she started school in Turkey and quickly became a celebrity and a peace icon, getting invited to various different events throughout the world, traveling far and wide, and disseminating both trips and awards online via Twitter.

Bana was invited at several venues to present her book in New York City in October 2017. In December of the same year, she published an article for *TIME* magazine (Alabed 2017b), highly publicized by the Office of the United Nations High Commissioner for Refugees (UNHCR 2017). Collaboration with mainstream media—on and offline—as well as with UN agencies is a further characteristic of the girl activists discussed in the present volume (see Chapters 2, 3, 4, 6, and 7). Bana was also invited onstage at the Oscars ceremony in February 2018, a photo of which has become her profile on Twitter ever since then (@AlabedBana). Shortly after, she received The Rising Star Award at the 8th Asian Awards in London, in April 2018, followed by the Freedom Award 2018 in Berlin on June 23 that year (Atlantic Council 2018). At the event, she was introduced by Nick Waters, Bellingcat Investigation Team and Finalist for European Press Prize, who was actually the person who carried out the investigation about her identity and geo-localization at a time of maximum speculation (Waters 2016). She was eventually invited to speak at the United Nations headquarters in NYC in September 2018: "My message to the @UN: peace for everyone. education for everyone" (@AlabedBana, 10:46—24 Sept. 2018; 249 RT—1465 likes). This call for universal education may well remind readers of Malala Yousafzai (see Chapter 2).

Being a guest speaker at the United Nations headquarters is a turning point in the career of a human rights activist, stepping onto the public arena, and at the United Nations no less. It is also an opportunity for her to enter the select few girls from the Global South who have actually managed to speak at the UN, publish their memoirs about their story of survival, and have gone on to become key icons in contemporary culture worldwide. Such are the stories of Malala, Hyeonseo, Yeonmi, Bana, and, as will be seen in the following chapters, Nujeen and Nadia. All these young women have been raised to prominence and given the right to speak out which is denied to many others. They reach their public on a first-name basis. Interestingly, they do so not only in an informal way managing their own personal social media platforms, but through renowned media and agencies, as is the case of the UN. Seeing this as an opportunity and not a re-traumatizing event or a silencing from the top down, I value the potential these stories told by girls in a testimonial fashion—in all aspects of the word—may yet have in shaping the future, discussing what each of us can do when faced with so much in the world that is not working. Bridging the eternal divide separating those in positions of relative power and those in the position of the Other, of discourses of victimization or hate, of "us" versus "them", narratives that aim at empathy and to foster awareness, though with their admitted failings, are necessary food for thought.

It is tweets like "My dream is to make the world a better place for all of us. Because i love all of you" (@AlabedBana, 10:20—16 Nov. 2018) that have turned Bana into a global peace icon. Most of the replies on Twitter comprise emoticons, with some sending hugs, huge hearts, and teddy bears, making use of a highly emotive language. That particular tweet has 67 replies, 140RT, and 1,1K likes. Going back to the beginning and coming full circle, one might argue that she is now, as she was during her time in Aleppo, an Internet sensation and a viral phenomenon. Now, her simple messages, typos included, are meant to strike a chord with those attuned. She persists in her message of love across borders and global friendship. In that sense, she fits the criteria of agencies like UNHCR, though of course she resorts to a childlike emotional discourse, not the typical way a life story mediated by UNHCR might see the light.[5] One just needs a glance at their website, newsletter, Twitter, Facebook, and so on, to notice the dramatic differences. Life stories mediated by

UNHCR take a divergent approach, a more nuanced, mature, reasoned take. Even if they highlight the plight of individuals, they do so via well-thought, well-prepared, professional writing and editing. Also when it is an audio, or an audiovisual reportage, much the same can be said. And yet, their goals are the same: bringing people's stories to light so that we can all empathize. Thus, the approaches, though quite different in nature, are compatible. They do not contradict each other. Rather, they offer a different view on the same issue. And they emphasize the deepest concern—that refugees are as human and therefore as in need of protection—as anybody else.

Finally, Bana was back in London for yet another award that year: the Youth Achievement Award at the Arab Women of the Year (MEMO 2018). The ceremony took place on 7 December 2018 at the Jumeirah Carlton Tower Hotel, London (Regent's 2018). Bana tweeted her gratitude to the organizers: "Happy. It's my honor to receive youth achievement award from London Arabia. Thank you so much" (@Alabed-Bana, 8 Dec. 2018). The photo reveals that, together with the London Arabia Organisation, presented on Twitter as "The Arab Women of the Year Awards, a prestigious new global celebration of achievement and excellence for Arab women" (@londonarabia 2018), the event was co-organized by UNHCR. This is highly relevant for the sake of my overarching project, as it brings together the young women activists this book discusses and I engage with. Their role in shaping public opinion, bringing to light personal stories of refugees, migrants, and other displaced people from across the world, is vital in getting others to care, to empathize, and perhaps change attitudes and public agendas. The activists this book comments on certainly strive to effect change on a global scale, as does UNHCR.

In spring 2019, Bana was invited to speak at the Global Education & Skills Forum, held in Dubai 22–24 March (@GESForum 2019). In her public intervention at the closing plenary session, she stressed the importance of education for victims of conflict as is the case of Syrian children. Addressing the audience, she spoke "about the need of education for the Syrian children. Syrian children will be a lost generation if they don't get education now" (@AlabedBana, 2:26—24 Mar. 2019). As the organization tweeted a few days later, in her speech Bana stressed the importance of education for children to have hope and dreams: "without education they don't want to be anything" (@GESForum, 3:00 PM—31 Mar. 2019). This message rings a bell to those attuned with Malala

Yousafzai's long-standing activism (Chapter 2), as well as that of Nujeen Mustafa, who will be the subject of the following chapter in this book (Chapter 6).

Images and Trauma

The centrality of imagery to convey trauma is also worth studying. A parallel between Bana's memoir (Alabed 2017a) and *The Raqqa Diaries: Escape from 'Islamic State'* (Salem 2017), both published in 2017, may be drawn. Interestingly, neither Alabed nor Salem acknowledge a co-author, ghostwriter, or otherwise. Both memoirs choose a very similar, compact format, and both were published the same year. Strategically, images have been chosen, curated, and placed in chronological order for the reader to better digest the book's contents. Bana's tweets are comparable to Salem's earlier short animated videos in that the visual is prominently presented for empathetic and ethical engagement, whereas the actual written words play a far less prominent role overall. These multimodal texts, I believe, may well be read at what Sidonie Smith and Julia Watson (2002) call the "visual/verbal interface" (37). Where Bana (Alabed 2017a) includes hand-drawn material, Salem (2017) works with comics panels, which likewise contain both visuals and words, with one necessarily needing the rest to be read together as a whole. Like diary entries, the messages compose a narrative in chronological order, providing evidence, photographic and otherwise, proper of citizen journalism, but more reliant on the emotions it excites. Importantly, in both Salem's and Bana's narratives, the major mediator has been BBC (2016a, b), whose publicity and dissemination of their written and audiovisual messages was an important step before they either achieved international acclaim and/or a book deal.

As Kay Schaffer and Sidonie Smith (2004) persuasively argue, stories of abuses deploy images to "put a human face to suffering" (3). It is a common trend, moreover, for human rights groups to use pictures of victimized or endangered women and children, a strategy that may in turn be criticized as it falls complicit into Sara Ahmed's (2004) "affective economies." But "though subject to political agendas, human rights life narratives are nonetheless those of vital voices and discourses that need to be heard, addressed, and redressed. Bana Alabed's tweets represent part of a trend to seek stories from children to denounce systemic causes of violation" (Martínez García 2017b, 137). And yet, being a life writer, her decision what to include and what to leave out of those images and words is a potentially empowering one. The interplay of the visual and verbal realm "fosters a strong emotional investment" (Martínez García 2017b, 145).

Already in 2016, Bana was tweeting about dead children in Idlib and posting disturbing photographs on Twitter:

> Went to school this morning and just now is killed by falling bombs in Idlib. Look his school bag OMG! I'm crying (@AlabedBana, 4:38 - 26 Oct. 2016; 96 replies—1111 RT—788 likes)

Her compelling tweets in February 2020 are yet again full of this visual imagery of the ravages of war and the impact on children's lives. Meant to move readers/audiences to rage, not to pity, they make for a shocking testimonial that is not first-hand, since Bana now tweets from Turkey, but relayed second-hand as if giving voice to the dead. It thus calls for immediate response and redress. The terrible succession of images of dead children is quite hard to witness to, even at a distance.

Strategic Use of Names

This chapter closes with a reflection on the uses of names. As happened with Zlata or Malala, Bana is mainly known by just her first name. Getting to know these girls on a first-name basis is crucial for the degree of empathizing that may be reached. It is a vital authorial strategy to generate strategic narrative empathy (Keen 2016). To date, Bana Alabed's life-writing project remains an understudied, complex example of how "emotionally charged" (Martínez García 2019a, 212) first-person testimony can be harnessed online and offline in advocacy campaigns. In fact, her personal webpage, created in 2018 after the release of her memoir, is precisely entitled just that—"Bana" (Alabed 2019a). This is an intriguing and complex new part of her ongoing life-writing project, one that has diversified over the years and with a particular goal to bring her close to her audience and potential readers. Thus, Bana seemingly sends postcards online via this platform. Accompanying each picture describing a happy event in her recent life as a peace activist is a short text one might well have expected on the back of an old-fashioned postcard. At the end of each short text is her signature—"Bana X" (Alabed 2019a). I find this strategy—relying on the affordance of "shareability" (Papacharissi 2012, 1992)—very successful in terms of getting the user to click on the next slide which immediately takes them to another event, another short text, the same face and the same signature.[6] By repeating very basic information, Bana remains true to her style, developed on Twitter since early on. By repeating her first name so often, she makes sure she is branding herself. She is very much aware by now of the brand she has created around her persona. There is no denying this is a conscious effort to build a future self. Each performance of the self on Twitter relates to a larger project of self-construction under way.

Bana makes an effort to identify herself every step of the way as the author of the book *Dear World: A Syrian Girl's Story of War and Plea for Peace* (Alabed 2017a). Not only does the book and its many translations appear in the background of her profile (@AlabedBana) on Twitter (Alabed 2016a), but she places special emphasis on this work on her personal website. It is to be noted that there are only four clickable sections on the top right-hand side of the page, and one is "BOOK" (Alabed 2019a). "ABOUT" provides a short bio, while "LATEST" refers to the aforementioned interesting digital postcards she sends. Last but not least, her Twitter account is just one click away, the icon placed right on the top right-hand side corner, making it easily discernible and accessible to all users, both experienced and inexperienced.

Attending to Genette's (1997) theory of "paratexts," the information on the cover raises certain expectations. One such expectation is the identification of author's name and image. In *Dear World* (Alabed 2017a), the name Bana Alabed occupies the upper section and is written in big block letters. Impossible to doubt the identification between that name and the girl in the picture, the ghostwriter is effaced and no information contradicts the authority of the claim, not even in the inner pages.

The title of Bana's book (Alabed 2017a) recalls the blogs Cardell (2014) discusses in her similarly titled *Dear World*. For Bana, these two words are emblematic of her tweets, with a great number of them starting that way, addressing a compassionate audience out there. Bana's editor is Christine Pride, based in the NYC headquarters of the firm (Kirkus 2018), who describes herself as interested in bringing new voices to the public and so not only edits but also does (ghost) writing of her own as well (Pride 2019). It is precisely Simon & Schuster Senior Editor at the time of publication who explicitly points out the similarities between Bana and Malala: "Recalling iconic young heroines such as Malala Yousafzai, Bana's experiences and message transcend the headlines and pierce through the political noise and debates to remind us of the human cost of war and displacement" (Simon & Schuster 2017). If Bana's life-writing project follows Malala's, one can argue their narratives are "co-constructed as family memoirs, then, geared at achieving the widest impact by maximizing the child figure – not just any child, but Ziauddin's and Fatemah's respectively – for political purposes" (Martínez García 2017b, 144).[7]

I end this chapter with a reflection on what seems to me a clear aesthetic of repetition,[8] carefully orchestrated so that what one can access online, via Twitter (Alabed 2016a), is replicated and multiplied on other media, be that Instagram (Alabed 2016b), the book (Alabed 2017a), her articles (Alabed 2017b), personal website (Alabed 2019a), or her YouTube channel (Alabed 2019b).

Notes

1. The chapter has been expanded, adapted, and updated from an original article on Bana Alabed (Martínez García 2017b). The manuscript first appeared online as "Bana Alabed: using Twitter to draw attention to human rights violations" and was later included in an issue of *Prose Studies* (2017), 39 (2–3): 132–149. https://doi.org/10.1080/01440357.2018.1549310 © 2018 Informa UK Limited, trading as Taylor & Francis Group.
2. For more on the interplay between children and humanitarian crisis narratives, see Whitlock (2007) and Douglas (2010).
3. For famous girl images in humanitarian campaigns, see Hariman and Lucaites (2007, 177–179), Whitlock (2007, 69–74), and Olesen (2016).
4. Twitter's decision to double its character count from 140 to 280 characters in 2017 has not made a real difference on the average length of a tweet (Perez 2018).
5. For more on the role of UNHCR in mediating refugee narratives, see Martínez García (2021).
6. For further technological affordances, see boyd (2010) and Papacharissi (2012).
7. See Douglas (2018) for more on Bana Alabed following the example of Malala Yousafzai.
8. For more on repetition as a vital activist strategy, see Martínez García (2020).

Works Cited

Ahmed, Sara. 2004. Affective Economies. *Social Text* 79 (22/2): 117–139.

Alabed, Bana. 2016a. @AlabedBana. *Twitter*, September. https://twitter.com/AlabedBana. Accessed 23 January 2020.

———. 2016b. @alabed_bana. *Instagram*, December. https://www.instagram.com/p/BOBA8QzA95j/. Accessed 23 January 2020.

———. 2017a. *Dear World: A Syrian Girl's Story of War and Plea for Peace*. London: Simon & Schuster.

———. 2017b. The World Can Be Doing More for Refugees. *TIME*, 18 December. https://time.com/5068581/bana-alabed-aleppo-syria-europe-refugees/. Accessed 24 January 2020.

———. 2019a. Bana. Personal webpage. https://bana-alabed.com/. Accessed 23 January 2020.

———. 2019b. Bana Alabed. YouTube channel. *YouTube*, 9 April. https://www.youtube.com/channel/UCl6kYciXdGb3QRycVvACQbw. Accessed 23 January 2020.

@garethicke. 2017. Fake Fake Fake Fake Fake Fake Fake. *Twitter*, 8 April. Web. Accessed 6 July 2017.

@gomgoor. 2017. Not ISIS, Another Rebels. *Twitter*, 7 April. Web. Accessed 6 July 2017.

@pinningjenny. 2017. This Is Pretty Hypocritical, Since Usually You Say You Want Peace. *Twitter*, 7 April. Web. Accessed 6 July 2017.

@Xerxesss. 2017. I Think This Account Belongs to ISIS. *Twitter*, 7 April. Web. Accessed 6 July 2017.

The Asian Awards. 2018. http://www.theasianawards.com/Bana_%20al_Abed.html. Accessed 8 May 2019.

Atlantic Council. 2018. https://www.atlanticcouncil.org/news/transcripts/2018-freedom-awards-bana-alabed. Accessed 8 May 2019.

BBC. 2016a. Animated diary: Life in Raqqa Under 'Islamic State.' *BBC News*, 29 February. https://www.bbc.com/news/video_and_audio/headlines/35684986/animated-diary-life-in-raqqa-under-islamic-state. Accessed 10 March 2020.

———. 2016b. Bana Alabed, Seven-Year-Old Tweeting from Aleppo, Goes Quiet. *BBC News*, 5 December. https://www.bbc.com/news/world-middle-east-38205889. Accessed 10 March 2020.

boyd, danah. 2010. Social Network Sites as Networked Publics: Affordances, Dynamics, and Implications. In *A Networked Self: Identity, Community, and Culture on Social Network Sites*, ed. Zizi Papacharissi, 39–58. New York: Routledge.

Cardell, Kylie. 2014. *Dear World: Contemporary Uses of the Diary*. Madison: University of Wisconsin Press.

Douglas, Kate. 2010. *Contesting Childhood: Autobiography, Trauma, and Memory*. New Brunswick: Rutgers University Press.

———. 2018. @Alabedbana: Twitter, the Child, and the War Diary. *Textual Practice*: 1–19. https://doi.org/10.1080/0950236X.2018.1533493.

Douglas, Kate, and Anna Poletti. 2016. *Life Narratives and Youth Culture: Representation, Agency and Participation*. London: Palgrave Macmillan.

Genette, Gérard. 1997. *Paratexts: Thresholds of Interpretation*, trans. Jane E. Lewin. Cambridge: Cambridge University Press.

Gibson, Caitlin. 2016. How a 7-Year-Old Aleppo Girl on Twitter Became Our Era's Anne Frank. *The Washington Post*, 6 December. https://www.washingtonpost.com/lifestyle/style/how-a-7-year-old-aleppo-girl-on-twitter-became-our-eras-anne-frank/2016/12/06/b474af5c-bb09-11e6-91ee-1adddfe36cbe_story.html. Accessed 23 January 2020.

Global Education & Skills Forum (@GESForum). 2019. *Twitter*, 24 March. https://twitter.com/GESForum/status/1109900226947620865. Accessed 23 January 2020.

Göksun, Yenal. 2015. Cyberactivism in Syria's War: How Syrian Bloggers Use the Internet for Political Activism. In *New Media Politics: Rethinking Activism and National Security in Cyberspace*, ed. Banu Baybars-Hawks, 39–64. Newcastle upon Thyne: Cambridge Scholars.

Gregoire, Carolyn. 2016. Why Girls So Often Assume the Role of Bearing Witness to War. *The Huffington Post*, 19 December. https://www.huffpost.com/entry/bana-al-abed-anne-frank-diaries_n_584ef0e3e4b0bd9c3dfdd594. Accessed 11 May 2017.

Hariman, Robert, and John Louis Lucaites. 2007. *No Caption Needed: Iconic Photographs, Public Culture, and Liberal Democracy*. Chicago: University of Chicago Press.

Horowitz, Sara R. 2012. Literary Afterlives of Anne Frank. In *Anne Frank Unbound: Media, Imagination, Memory*, ed. Barbara Kirschenblatt-Gimblet and Jeffrey Shandler, 215–253. Bloomington: Indiana University Press.

Keen, Suzanne. 2016. Life Writing and the Empathetic Circle. *Concentric: Literary and Cultural Studies* 42 (2): 9–26.

Kirkus. 2018. Q&A: Christine Pride, a Senior Editor at Simon & Schuster. *Kirkus Reviews*, 8 August. https://www.kirkusreviews.com/features/christine-pride-simon-schuster/. Accessed 8 May 2019.

London Arabia Organisation. 2018. @londonarabia. *Twitter*, 7 December. https://twitter.com/londonarabia/status/1071143454988754945. Accessed 23 January 2020.

Martínez García, Ana Belén. 2016. Narrative Emotions and Human Rights Life Writing. In *On the Move: Glancing Backwards to Build a Future in English Studies*, ed. Aitor Ibarrola-Armendariz and Jon Ortiz de Urbina Arruabarrena, 127–132. Bilbao: University of Deusto.

———. 2017a. Unearthing the Past: Bringing Ideological Indoctrination to Light in North Korean Girls' Memoirs. *a/b: Auto/Biography Studies* 32 (3): 587–602.

———. 2017b. Bana Alabed: Using Twitter to Draw Attention to Human Rights Violations. *Prose Studies: History, Theory, Criticism* 39 (2–3): 132–149.

———. 2018. TED Talks as Life Writing: Online and Offline Activism. *Life Writing* 15 (4): 487–503.

———. 2019a. Construction and Collaboration in Life-Writing Projects: Malala Yousafzai's Activist 'I'. *Journal of Writing in Creative Practice* 12 (1 & 2): 201–217.

———. 2019b. Denouncing Human Trafficking in China: North Korean Women's Memoirs as Evidence. *State Crime Journal* 8 (1): 59–79.

———. 2020. Women Activists' Strategies of Online Self-Presentation. *AI & Society: Journal of Knowledge, Culture and Communication*. Special Issue on Iteration as Persuasion in a Digital World. Forthcoming.

———. 2021. Refugees' Mediated Narratives in the Public Sphere. *Narrative*. Special Issue on Narrative in the Public Sphere. Forthcoming.

McNeill, Laurie. 2014. Life Bytes: Six-Word Memoir and the Exigencies of Auto/Tweetographies. In *Identity Technologies: Constructing the Self Online*, ed. Anna Poletti and Julie Rak, 144–164. Madison: University of Wisconsin Press.

Middle East Monitor (MEMO). 2018. https://www.middleeastmonitor.com/20181225-bana-alabed-receives-arab-woman-of-the-year-award-in-london/. Accessed 8 May 2019.

Moore-Gilbert, Bart. 2009. *Postcolonial Life-Writing: Culture, Politics and Self-Representation*. Abingdon: Routledge.

Office of the United Nations High Commissioner for Refugees (UNHCR). 2017. *Facebook*, 26 December. https://www.facebook.com/UNHCR/posts/do-you-know-our-crimes-just-that-we-were-born-in-syria-the-world-can-do-better-a/10157214979438438/. Accessed 24 January 2020.

Olesen, Thomas. 2016. Malala and the Politics of Global Iconicity. *The British Journal of Sociology* 67 (2): 307–327.

Papacharissi, Zizi. 2012. Without You, I'm Nothing: Performances of the Self on Twitter. *International Journal of Communication* 6: 1989–2006.

———. 2015. Affective Publics and Structures of Storytelling: Sentiment, Events and Mediality. *Information, Communication & Society*: 1–18.

Perez, Sarah. 2018. Twitter's Doubling of Character Count from 140 to 280 Had Little Impact on Length of Tweets. *Tech Crunch*, 30 October. https://techcrunch.com/2018/10/30/twitters-doubling-of-character-count-from-140-to-280-had-little-impact-on-length-of-tweets/?guccounter=1&guce_referrer=aHR0cHM6Ly93d3cuZ29vZ2xlLmNvbS8&guce_referrer_sig=AQAAANdfJUDKg2TmPnY8ndzx_ZOdytFFZR54xh5clkYVLs4b5VsPJJ5U5e

SXVAmhLpLZ246L-Fg6FJK4mqVODQnlaYhvr3qW0M54WJnqb1FcYJj6tn4bfwwQ5fOwhoLPNKR9NIOwARshk1agzG_ZVpumdvtDGfbZav0l2bBUKz4Pf95M. Accessed 3 November 2018.

Pride, Christine. 2019. Christine Pride. Personal webpage. http://www.christinepride.com/. Accessed 8 May 2019.

Prose, Francine. 2015. Writing from a War Zone Doesn't Make You Anne Frank. *Foreign Policy*, 15 May. https://foreignpolicy.com/2015/05/15/writing-from-a-war-zone-doesnt-make-you-anne-frank-girl-emulated-farah-baker-zlata-filipovic/. Accessed 10 March 2020.

Regent's University London. 2018. 2018 Arab Women of the Year Award winners announced. *Regent's*, 7 December. https://www.regents.ac.uk/news/2018-arab-women-of-the-year-award-winners-announced. Accessed 23 January 2020.

Salem. 2017. *The Raqqa Diaries: Escape from 'Islamic State'*. London: Hutchinson.

Schaffer, Kay, and Sidonie Smith. 2004. *Human Rights and Narrated Lives: The Ethics of Recognition*. New York: Palgrave Macmillan.

Simon & Schuster. 2017. Simon & Schuster to Publish Book by Seven-Year-Old Syrian Girl Bana Alabed. 12 April. https://about.simonandschuster.biz/news/bana-alabed/. Accessed 13 June 2017.

Smith, Sidonie. 2006. Narratives and Rights: *Zlata's Diary* and the Circulation of Stories of Suffering Ethnicity. *WSQ: Women's Studies Quarterly* 34 (1–2): 133–152.

Smith, Sidonie, and Julia Watson. 2002. *Interfaces: Women, Autobiography, Image, Performance*. Ann Arbor: University of Michigan Press.

Waters, Nick. 2016. Finding Bana—Proving the Existence of a 7-Year-Old Girl in Eastern Aleppo. *Bellingcat*, 14 December. https://www.bellingcat.com/news/mena/2016/12/14/bana-alabed-verification-using-open-source-information/. Accessed 16 June 2017.

Whitlock, Gillian. 2007. *Soft Weapons: Autobiography in Transit*. Chicago: University of Chicago Press.

Wolf, Hope. 2015. 'Paper Is Patient': Tweets from the '#Annefrank of Palestine'. *Textual Practice* 29 (7): 1355–1374.

CHAPTER 6

Nujeen Mustafa: Syrian Refugee Defying Labels on TEDx

Abstract This chapter is the perfect companion to the preceding one, as it features the case of a Syrian girl who also left the country under strenuous circumstances and relocated as refugee elsewhere. Both life-writing projects may be read side by side to gauge the strategies at work by these two activists whose competing title as "the girl from Aleppo" is at stake. Instead of precluding each other's testimony, their voices denounce the situation in Syria and the individual and collective ramifications of leaving their country behind. Born with cerebral palsy, Nujeen Mustafa's journey into Europe was featured by mainstream media. Nujeen—also a household name—is most famous for her public speeches advocating for the need to move beyond labeling people as numbers, migrants, refugees.

Keywords Nujeen Mustafa · Refugee · Labels · Aleppo · Syria · Public speeches

Nujeen Mustafa is a young woman who, aged 16, escaped Syria with the help of her sister who pushed her wheelchair all the way until their arrival in Germany. Now an icon for the rights of refugees and disabled people (she was born with cerebral palsy), she came into the spotlight upon her crossing the Mediterranean in a rubber dinghy. Her experience of migration was featured by multiple media outlets which followed her advances and final relocation.

A. B. Martínez García, *New Forms of Self-Narration*, Palgrave Studies in Life Writing, https://doi.org/10.1007/978-3-030-46420-2_6

The (Other) Girl from Aleppo

This chapter is the perfect companion to the preceding chapter, devoted to Bana Alabed (Chapter 5), as it features the case of a further Syrian girl—Nujeen Mustafa—who also comes from Aleppo, left the country under strenuous circumstances, and relocated as refugee elsewhere. In a way, both life-writing projects may be read side by side to gauge the strategies at work by these two activists whose competing title as "the girl from Aleppo" is at stake.

BBC correspondent Fergal Keane first interviewed Nujeen Mustafa on 16 September 2015 as she was "making the long journey to a new life through Croatia with her sister" (BBC News 2015a). In the title to that video report, BBC called her a "disabled Syrian *teenager*" (BBC News 2015a; emphasis added). Just a few days later, on 19 September 2016, Philip Oltermann writes for *The Guardian* an interview with the then 17-year-old entitled "'I hope Merkel keeps us': How Nujeen Mustafa traveled from Syria to Germany in a wheelchair" where he calls her a "young refugee" (Oltermann 2016). But once the memoir (Mustafa and Lamb 2016) is released on 22 September 2016, paradoxically, her age goes seemingly backward, as the publishers decide to call her a "girl" in the title (Mustafa and Lamb 2016). Similarly, Simon Worrall, writing for *National Geographic* on November 6, also calls her a "girl" (Worrall 2016). Asked whether Nujeen is "the new Malala" (Worrall 2016), co-author Christina Lamb jokingly replies she is making a career out of writing about 16- and 17-year-old strong women. The buildup toward Nujeen's claim to girlhood—and thus to being known just on a first-name basis as has been seen in other chapters (see Chapters 2 and 5)—was complete once a revised edition of her memoir was published on 10 October 2017 entitled *The Girl from Aleppo* (Mustafa and Lamb 2017). Was this change of title made on purpose, to compete for the title of "girl from Aleppo" that was arguably already in possession of Bana Alabed? Interestingly, the release of a picture book on Bana Alabed's life (Lorraine 2017) and Nujeen Mustafa's second revised edition of her memoir (Mustafa and Lamb 2017) was apparently simultaneous. Did the authors/editors/publishers/managers know and adapted titles accordingly?

Not only have Bana and Nujeen published a memoir, but major publishing houses have provided a venue—Simon & Schuster and William Collins. Bana's so-called memoir is admittedly a print publication of her tweets plus various diary-like materials, some photographs, and collages (Alabed 2017). Nujeen's memoir (Mustafa and Lamb 2017) fits the criteria of what one expects of human rights activists' memoirs: a strong cover, a compelling title, many photographs in the middle pages, a clear map of the area at the beginning, and sections with self-explanatory titles. In Nujeen's memoir, the Prologue is devoted to "The Crossing" (Mustafa and Lamb 2017, 1–8), the event that has effectively transformed her into a refugee. Even if her journey had started earlier, when forced to flee Aleppo due to the approach of Daesh,[1] it is not until she gets on the dinghy that she becomes one of the many refugees entering Europe in what was called at the time, and to a lesser extent continues to be called, the "migrant crisis." The fact that Nujeen chooses this event to frame the narrative is clearly strategic. Even though she may display a conflicting attitude toward the term "refugee" as will be seen throughout this chapter, she is also an activist for the rights of refugees, so, by starting the memoir with the experience of crossing the Mediterranean, she situates the reader straightaway in the focal point of her life story and advocacy.

Bana Alabed has received several awards (see Chapter 5), but Nujeen Mustafa actually made it to the list of 100 most influential women in the world by the BBC in 2018. In place 69 of 100, she is celebrated for her sustained, impactful activism for disabled refugees (BBC News 2018). Christina Lamb, her co-author, tweeted about it (@christinalamb, 20 Nov. 2018), and Nujeen retweeted, as is her norm, without adding any self-praise to the message, letting the facts speak for themselves. If at all, she might reply with an embarrassed-looking emoticon, as her reply to @girleffect the previous day shows (@NujeenMustafa, 10:16—19 Nov. 2018).

Fruit of her long-running collaboration with Football Club Barcelona, Nujeen Mustafa was awarded the 2019 International Cule Award on 14 February 2019. Nujeen retweeted the photographs and message from the Barça Foundation praising her #CulerdelAny award: "Felicitats a tots els premiats a la gala #CulerdelAny del @sport. En especial a @Nujeen-Mustafa" (@FundacioFCB, 15 Feb. 2019), as well as an enthusiastic tweet from her co-author: "Not everyday you see a friend replacing Messi on the front of Barcelona's main sports paper. Wow @NujeenMustafa" (@christinalamb, 15 Feb. 2019). This follows FCB campaign #NoChild-Offline, where she was featured alongside another refugee teenage girl, Givara Khalil, to advocate in favor of women's rights and access to health care and sports for refugees, addressing the inequality and hardship endured due to their lack of status and of physical documentary proof of who they were (@FundacioFCB, 9 Jan. 2019).[2] This is an aspect of the paradox of unidentified migrants' experiences that weighs heavily in Nujeen's mind and that she is keen on exploring in her public speeches and constant acts of self-construction on and offline.

Nujeen Mustafa is also the 2019 Recipient of the Alison Des Forges Award for Extraordinary Activism (HRW 2019). In the announcement, Human Rights Watch emphasizes her commitment to speak out for the rights of refugees and people with disabilities, so it fits the criteria of an award celebrating "the valor of people who put their lives on the line to protect the dignity and rights of others" (HRW 2019). Indeed, her advocacy campaign, mainly distributed online via videos shared on multiple platforms—NGO websites, YouTube, Twitter—has opened the door to policy changes in the European Union:

> In a unique partnership with Human Rights Watch, the European Disability Forum, and the Norwegian Refugee Council, Mustafa urged senior policymakers in the European Union to re-evaluate their policies regarding people with disabilities in humanitarian crises. The EU commissioner for humanitarian assistance has announced new measures to ensure that the delivery of humanitarian aid meets the needs of people with disabilities. (HRW 2019)

This important award, the public recognition that comes with it, as well as the potential implementation of actual measures within the EU policy toward people with disabilities, is a significant step forward in Nujeen's activism. Furthermore, it is proof that life writing, broadly understood, may shape people's consciousness, encourage empathy, and so eventually lead to social justice.

Commodified or Mediatized?

With Kate Douglas and Anna Poletti (2016), this section, much as the following ones, begs the question: "To what extent do young writers exert agency in the production, circulation and reception of their life narratives?" (226). As in other activist life-writing projects, Nujeen exemplifies the "I" of a "powerful agent" (Martínez García 2019a, 204), which makes use of available templates and circuits of distribution to reach ever wider publics. By refusing to conform to the narrative others prepare for her, she exercises the agency expected of an empowered self.

At the height of the 2015 migrant crisis, Nujeen Mustafa's story attracted mainstream and alternative news media alike. Nujeen compiles in her memoir the exact figures relating her sister's and her own journey (Mustafa and Lamb 2017, 279–284). In the Appendix, she presents the data matter-of-factly: "Total distance 3593 miles, total travel cost 5045 euros (for me and my sister)" (279). Crucially, she includes the time she spent as an internally displaced person in Manbij, which makes for over two years (27 July 2012–Aug. 2014). In comparison, the time spent in Turkey, as opposed to other refugees' stories, is significantly shorter, not even two weeks. Once in Europe, she crossed from Greece into Macedonia, from there to Serbia, was refused entry at the border with Hungary, moved on to Croatia, then Slovenia, Austria, and finally Germany. Throughout the journey, she was lucky enough to only be detained twice, for a total of two days, in Slovenia, one day held in a cell at a police station (Mustafa and Lamb 2017, 192–193), another day inside a detention center (195–201).

Media attention devoted to Nujeen's journey has been summarized by *New York Times* reporter Robert Mackey (2015). Nujeen's arrival in Lesbos was captured by Irish photographer Ivor Prickett working for the Office of the United Nations High Commissioner for Refugees (UNHCR), who uploaded the photographic evidence onto Instagram (Mackey 2015). Prickett interviewed her and was surprised to hear her fluent English and resilient positive attitude toward the crossing. Just two weeks later, as Hungary closed its border with Serbia, she was interviewed for the BBC by Fergal Keane, whom she told she wanted to be an astronaut (BBC News 2015b). The very same day, ABC News also featured her interview with Mary Bruce, where she talked of her favorite American soap opera, *Days of Our Lives* (@marykbruce, 12:59 a.m., 17 Sept. 2015). The following day—not "days later" as argued by Mackey (2015)—Keane found her in a detention camp in Slovenia (@BBCWorld, 18 Sept. 2015). When Keane caught up with her again, she and her sister were already in Germany, reunited with her brother (Robin Show 2015). As *The New York Times* article goes on to explain, the impact of having a US media giant—HBO—featuring her story was tremendous. With over 11,096,059 views, this video is one of the most-watched ones where Nujeen's life is discussed (Last Week 2015). ABC also went to see her at the Essen refugee camp where she was awaiting her documentation to show her the clip proving the actors had momentarily reunited for her sake (Bruce et al. 2015). In thanks, she replied with a YouTube video link via Twitter (@NujeenMustafa, 13:23—29 Sept. 2015). From the beginning, then, her use of social media was apparently multiplatform-based.

The intensive coverage of Nujeen's journey reminds readers/audiences of the "commodification of sensationalized life narratives by Arab and Muslim women" (Whitlock 2007, 117) and their market circulation. Nujeen's memoir (Mustafa and Lamb 2016) was among the *Sunday Times* 2016 books of the year (Patterson 2016).[3] In her memoir, first published in October 2016, republished a year later (Mustafa and Lamb 2017), Nujeen recounts her harrowing journey. Though the two editions are separated by less than a year, they diverge in form. First and foremost, they show a different take on both cover and title, with a clear exchange of the word "wheelchair" in the first title for an image on the cover in the second edition and the telling appearance of words like "girl" and "escape" in the latter to highlight, as has been previously done, the plight of the girl of humanitarian discourse (Hesford and Kozol 2005). Drawing on Gérard Genette's (1997) notion of "paratexts," I aim to shed light on the strategic narrative empathizing techniques (Keen 2008, 2016) that underlie these conscious editorial decisions.

Images are placed in the middle pages (Mustafa and Lamb 2017, 162i–viii), combining pictures of her growing up and her family—as if taken from her family album—as well as others obtained from various media outlets on the city of Aleppo and Syria as a whole. The affective power of these images is unquestionable. In the words of Judith Butler (2005), a "political battle … is taking place in part through the medium of the visual image" (827). Moreover, "Here, as elsewhere in the era of humanitarianism and human rights, images of children and lost childhoods are invoked to shame individuals, communities, nations, and that imagined 'international community' into action" (Smith 2006, 145). The captions that accompany Mustafa's photographs use an eloquent, emphatic, and vivid style, capturing Mustafa's voice and her vindications, as if one could hear her speak while reading: "an awful massacre" (Mustafa and Lamb 2017, 162ii), "we had great hopes but they soon faded" (162iii), "Tired, bored and wanting to see my brother!" (162vi), "Reunited!" (162vii), "I miss them terribly" (162viii).

As mentioned earlier, Nujeen's co-author—Christina Lamb—is the same as Malala's (Chapter 2), and Malala herself contributes to the publicizing of Nujeen's work both on digital platforms (epitext) and offline, by writing the blurb on both covers (peritext) praising her and inviting everyone to read her story. Two blurbs appear above and below the title of the 2017 edition (Mustafa and Lamb 2017) which grab readers' attention. Right above the title come Malala's words praising the specific girl in the story: "She is our hero. Everyone must read her story. She will inspire you." While these words are more centered on the character of the girl narrator activist, the following blurb refers to the story in broader terms, highlighting the universality of its claims. Thus, *The Sunday Times* writes: "Extraordinary ... An important chronicle of our strange and terrible times." At once, two types of the strategic empathizing techniques Suzanne Keen (2016) talks about are activated: On the one hand, the story is portrayed as a very personal narrative of ethnic suffering—what Keen (2016) calls "ambassadorial strategic empathy" (20); on the other hand, a claim of universality guarantees shared affects and interests—what Keen (2016) calls "broadcast strategic empathy" (22).

The first edition of Nujeen Mustafa's memoir (Mustafa and Lamb 2016) was released on 22 September 2016 by renowned publishing house William Collins, an imprint of HarperCollins, over one year after Hyeonseo Lee's (Chapter 3) memoir (Lee and John 2015)—released by William Collins on 2 July 2015. In their description of this imprint, HarperCollins emphasizes the role that tradition plays, with a long history of publishing devoted to nonfiction, but at the same time interested in innovative and inspirational authors (HarperCollins 2019). It is an undeniable trend nowadays for major transnational agencies, news media, publishing houses, and other actors in the public sphere to both engage with and feature life writing by young women from the Global South who, in turn, become global activists. Coincidences are evident, signaling not just a development in how human rights activism works, but also how youth activism, feminist activism, and life writing work. They are enmeshed in contemporary culture, a culture of denunciation across borders and of multiplatform ubiquity (see Martínez García 2020).

Dismantling Stereotypes

In what follows, I track the narrating "I"s in Nujeen's life-writing project, with a special focus on her memoir and the ways the pronoun switches for strategic narrative purposes.

In pages 13–21 of Nujeen Mustafa's memoir (Mustafa and Lamb 2017), the narrating "I" that asserts "The first fact to know about me is I'm a Kurd" (13) is mostly overcome by the collective consciousness of "we Kurds" (15). Thus, her Kurdish "I" is central to her identity. She explains their history, and how being a Kurd has both positive and negative effects. On the one hand, she argues women are freer than those from other Muslim strands (Mustafa and Lamb 2017, 14). On the other hand, she insists they have been suffering at the hands of states for generations (15–17, 35–38, 53–58). Nujeen adopts quite a didactic tone to emphasize the richness of their culture and the hatred and victimization they have suffered throughout history (15–17). Kurds are, as the title of Chapter 1 in her memoir reads, "Foreigners in Our Own Land" (11). Nujeen aims at dismantling stereotypes, for instance when she discusses so-called "Arab heroes" (16), who are, in fact, Kurd. She denounces Syrian authorities forcing them to speak Arabic and not issuing them ID cards, effectively depriving them of citizenship and thus of the right to ownership, to have a government job, to vote, or to attend high school (16). Turkey, however, is worse, according to Nujeen: "Turkey is the hardest place to be a Kurd" (17). Among all the oddities she mentions, is the fact that people have been imprisoned for using the Kurdish alphabet: "until not long ago you could be arrested there if you used the letters Q, W and X, which don't exist in the Turkish language. Imagine going to jail for a consonant!" (17). As is typical with all the human rights activists contained within these pages, emphasis is laid on key phrases and geared at exciting an emotional and ethical reaction from readers/audiences. Nujeen's emphatic use of the exclamation mark in the extract above, which reminds readers of her TEDx talks, makes a strong call for attention.

Images play a prominent role in testimonial accounts and this is no exception. Imbued of affective power, the audiovisual text of Nujeen's TED talks (Mustafa 2017, 2018), as much as other young women activists' TED talks (see Martínez García 2018), is highly reliant on images, both still—on PowerPoint slides—and moving—the speaker herself in front of the audience. The text must therefore be read at the "visual/verbal interface" (Smith and Watson 2002, 37): "Directing attention to the interfaces of autobiographical acts illuminates how they affect or mobilize meanings: the textual can set in motion certain readings of the image; and the image can then revise, retard, or reactivate that text" (21). Reading the memoir, one is informed of the context, which makes for a more affective reading of the photographs contained in its middle pages (Mustafa and Lamb 2017, 162i–viii). At the same time, the pictures revise stereotypes associated with Syrian girlhood, with Muslim girls and women showing their hair without using a veil, effectively defying preconceptions of Muslim identity politics: "We are Muslims too but not so rigid. In the high school my sisters and cousins were the only girls who didn't cover their heads" (14). Nujeen makes sure to emphasize from the very beginning how being a Kurd trumps being a Muslim, making a claim not to be confused with extremists, a further shared feature with Malala. In fact, Nujeen's open denunciation of Daesh's practices of indoctrination (Mustafa and Lamb 2017, 92–94) harks back to those of the Taliban as described in Malala's memoir, as both extremist groups make sure to appear peaceful and to seduce children with gifts and kindness so as to count with their support later on once the violence starts. After crimes committed in the name of jihad, Nujeen asks the question: "How could these people say they were for Islam?" (Mustafa and Lamb 2017, 94) which, again, reminds readers of a very similar question posed by Malala (Chapter 2). Both Malala and Nujeen emphasize—Nujeen less often as it is not the purpose of the memoir—Islam as a religion of peace and how that clashes dramatically with extremist interpretations. Instead, Nujeen's "I" is a political "I" when she chooses which name to call the rebel terrorist group who has driven them from their home: "I refuse to call them Islamic State as who said they are a state? Can I just become Nujeen State? Of course not!" (117). Her mocking tone is accompanied of an ethical call for awareness and bears some reflection on what (potentially damaging) effects the choice of a name, be that "ISIS" or "refugee," may have on other people.

The complex emotions Nujeen shows, from enthusiasm to guilt and back, might be associated with the state of mind of a teenager. Some extracts read like stream of consciousness, such as the following on her competing thoughts and emotions pulling her in different directions at the same time: "I was excited to see another country, even though I felt guilty ... and happy to see ..." (187). This mood swing does not surprise anyone familiar with teenagers or who looks back on how their thought process usually went along those years. In Zagreb, Nujeen has a lot of first-time experiences in a day, both good and bad. First, at her "*first ever* McDonald's" she dislikes the food and, especially, the drinks: "My Coke was bubbly, which I don't really like" (189; emphasis added). Next, she rejoices in other things that take her by surprise:

> we went to a shopping mall, *my first* one, and I had *another first* too – *my first* time on an escalator. We spent a long time trying to work out how to use it in a wheelchair. *It was awesome*, though a little bit scary on the way down. (190; emphasis added)

The repetition and emphatic style make these phrases a clear example of a teenage narrating "I." The Postscript closes on a similar note, with phrases like "That's cool" and "can't wait" closely followed by "I am still cross" (269). Faced with such an internal clash of emotions, one remembers too well one's own teenage years, particularly with her matter-of-fact confession: "My family say I overreact and am too dramatic about things but it's not easy being a teenager" (271). Thus, she justifies the contradictions that populate her pages.

"I hate" is one of the expressions Nujeen repeats the most in her memoir. Nujeen's hating "I" is like Bana's (Chapter 5) and shows some lack of maturity on her part. Nujeen's tirade against history books and media glorifying tyrants or "bad guys" (59), with direct mention of Syrian President Bashar al-Assad or "Assad" for short (60), also reminds readers of other activists, like Yeonmi Park from Chapter 4 in the present volume, and her rant against media attention on Kim Jong-un. Chapter 3 (35–44) in Nujeen's memoir is, similarly, full of hatred. Discussing Saddam Hussein's genocide of the Kurds on "Bloody Friday" (35) in 1998, she says:

> I hate that day – I wish I could delete it from the calendar. Saddam was an even worse dictator than Assad. Yet the West kept supporting Saddam for years, even giving him weapons. Sometimes it seems that nobody likes the Kurds. Our list of sorrows is endless. (36)

Yet, much as Nujeen identifies with being a Kurd, she dislikes some of her own traditions, as they involve large gatherings where she is never made to feel comfortable:

> To be honest, sometimes I hoped it would be banned because I hated going to it. First it was almost like torture to get me down those five floors of stairs. Then when we got there it was totally loud and crowded, and so uncomfortable sitting on the hard ground. I couldn't even see the folk dancing or the march with our national songs. And we had to be careful what we said because among the revellers were vendors selling balloons and ice-cream and candyfloss and people thought they were spies for Assad's intelligence. (37)

Perhaps Nujeen's misgivings are more to do with fear—of being fined or imprisoned—and agony at her disability than anything else. Similarly, her disgust for her brother Mustafa's impending wedding (44) can neither be detached from the fear that he, like his elder sisters before him, might leave her behind.

Apart from conflict raged between hatred and joy, the narrating "I" struggles to cope with many other universal emotions, among them: nostalgia, guilt, fear, worry, and hope (Mustafa and Lamb 2017, 267). This explicit—and repetitive—mention of the full range of emotions she continues to experience makes a bid for attention and shows authorial strategic empathy. To be more precise, appealing to universals is part of a "broadcast" narrative empathizing strategy (Keen 2016, 22) by which the narrating "I" emphasizes what all humans, independently of age, gender, religious, geopolitical, ethnic, class, or social group, share.

Disability is a core part of Nujeen's identity. She struggles to cope with her disabled "I" while at the same time embracing what it can offer. Chapter 2 in her memoir, entitled "The Walls of Aleppo" (Mustafa and Lamb 2017, 23–33), apparently describes this old, historical, beautiful city. However, it soon becomes clear as one continues reading that the reason for the title is that it works as a metaphor for her condition. After explaining she suffers from "a kind of cerebral palsy" (Mustafa and Lamb 2017, 24), she describes how her limbs may move of their own accord at any given time (23), so she feels trapped in her own body. The metaphor may even apply to the walls of the fifth-floor apartment where she lives in Aleppo, which isolate her from the rest of her family and friends, since she cannot easily go up and down the stairs and is therefore left out of school and games. Furthermore, the wall metaphor is a reflection of the isolation from the outside world experienced as a child, never fitting in with other children:

> I loved them, but whenever we played games I always felt like the weakest link and often they ran away from me, laughing as I tried to drag myself after them in my odd way *like a rabbit*. I looked *like a rabbit* with my teeth and I crawl-jumped *like a rabbit*… I was neither comfortable nor welcomed in the kids' world. (26; emphasis added)

The insistence in repeating the phrase "like a rabbit" shows not Nujeen's view of herself, but rather the words that must have been thrown at her as the sort of childish language that can so hurt other children growing up at a disadvantage.

Instead of physical contact, Nujeen says in her memoir that she used to have fun with first a TV, then a satellite dish, finally a computer (26): "Once I could read, my world was books, TV and sitting on the balcony" (28). Her self-taught initiative, watching documentaries for hours on end, and a potentially gifted mind with an impressive memory for numbers, made her a fast learner who, looking back, rues a lost, or rather never existent, childhood: "I was born with the mind of an adult" (33). This is by no means an unimportant detail in Nujeen's or other young women activists' life-writing projects: "Key to understanding the emotional currency of these narratives is their description of childhood as something the authors were robbed of" (Martínez García 2017a, 598).[4] Yet, Nujeen is angry at being looked down on because of how she looks, how she talks, and how she moves and, most especially, for the utter lack of privacy (32). This anger is a further universal emotion as the ones commented earlier, a normal part of struggling to cope with the reality of not being able to be totally independent from others' help or others' gaze.

Some passages focus on the crudeness of dependence. One such episode takes place when Nujeen's group is waiting to be boarded onto the dinghy: "It was decided that if the wheelchair became a problem in the boat we would get rid of it. No one said what would happen to me" (135). Her matter-of-fact tone impacts the reader strongly, laying bare the dehumanization that speech may encapsulate and bear down on others, and how easily one may unwittingly inflict pain on others (see Butler 2004). Nujeen confesses to feeling sad as they were nearing their final destination and projects what she saw as her potential future, much like her life in Aleppo: "I would go back to being the girl in her room" (Mustafa and Lamb 2017, 211). Living in confinement—or semi-confinement—due to her disability is a drawback that she wishes would go away. As she explained in her TEDx talk "My journey from Syria to Germany in a wheelchair" (Mustafa 2018), the journey was "like a dream" and she had "approached it with a six-year-old's curiosity," never wishing for it to end.

On many other occasions, however, Nujeen embraces the positive side of disability, deploying humor with a penchant for irony and a sardonic tint, among which feature references to Heidi and her friend Clara: "I didn't walk. I wish I could. Maybe I need a Peter to toss away my wheelchair" (213). In her memoir, Nujeen talks of what she calls "disability benefits" (Mustafa and Lamb 2017, 90) by which she unabashedly admits to getting her way pretty much every time there is a disagreement with her siblings, be that a book to read (90), a remote to control (45), and so on. Without saying so, she admits to being somewhat spoiled. It is hard to assess how this special treatment she was used to receiving may have affected her siblings in return. Watching Nasrine on the cover pushing Nujeen's wheelchair, for example, the humor Nujeen displays seems to be lost in the elder sibling's dutiful face and actions. Quite troubling is Nujeen's confession that continuing the journey throughout Europe, when faced with the choice between flying and traveling by land, she chose for them to take the road: "It would be hard for Nasrine pushing me but lots of fun. And for once I would be *like everyone else*" (Mustafa and Lamb 2017, 165; emphasis added). Paradoxically, the freer Nujeen feels, the more is needed from her companion. "Disability benefits" reappear along the journey, whenever Nujeen is helped by strangers (152, 175, 204). But, overall, her wish to be normal is at the heart of how she describes herself and her ambitions, such as "being an astronaut or walking" (244). Normalcy is not an uncommon ambition for a disabled person. Indeed, it builds upon the fact that she needs to be fully recognized as a person, not as a thing, an animal, or a statistic.

In "I Am Not a Number" Nujeen describes how helpless she felt right before the crossing: "All I heard was our group arguing over whether we should bring the wheelchair or not" (Mustafa 2017). At that point of her TEDx talk, photographs provide the visual testimony necessary to back up her claims. The witnessing audience is faced with a problematic ethical question—how difficult it must have been to cross the Mediterranean on a rubber dinghy with a metal wheelchair and being pushed by her sister—unacknowledged in the TEDx talk (Mustafa 2017), unlike in her memoir (Mustafa and Lamb 2017). In her second TEDx talk, Nujeen advocates more assertively for disabled people as capable of defining who they are (Mustafa 2018). Like the other young women in this volume, she insists on the importance of public self-presentation and recognition while reminiscing the moment she was approached to write a book: "this was my chance. This was my chance to tell people who I am, to tell the world who I am, every part of it: the Kurdish girl, the disabled girl, the refugee, the Federer fan, the Barça fan… All of it." All these parts of her identity, intertwined, are thus presented as one inseparable, complex self, a human being, both in the memoir (Mustafa and Lamb, 2017) and in the talk (Mustafa 2018).

Apart from bearing witness to Daesh and to disability on a quite personal form, Nujeen bears witness to the plight of people on the move who are devoid of rights. To denounce their dehumanization, she deploys the collective witnessing pronouns expected of *testimonio* (Beverley 1987). One of the most dramatic passages in Nujeen's memoir revolves around the time spent at the closed border between Serbia and Hungary. She recounts how she and her sister were pushed around against a barbed-wire fence and violently interviewed for Hungarian TV (Mustafa and Lamb 2017, 180), a day when violence escalated until a climactic point, with Hungarian riot police attacking refugees. Nujeen's "I" encompasses the plight of refugees as it switches into a denouncing "we":

> we watched as a column of armoured vehicles arrived on the Hungarian side. Hundreds more riot police emerged and started turning water cannon and teargas on the people protesting at the border…
>
> Afterwards the police claimed that 'aggressive' migrants had been breaking through the fence 'armed with pipes and sticks', but we didn't see anything like that, only people throwing plastic water bottles. (181)

The deployment of the witness "we" is key to how one reads the extract. The assertion that what is denounced has been seen—or not—supplies the authenticity required to bear witness to a crime and the ethical urgency of an issue not yet solved.

Using Online and Offline Advocacy for Rights Activism

Nujeen's TEDx talks, her tweets, her interviews, and her memoir, in short, all her life-writing texts, combine her two main causes for narrating her activist self: the rights of people—not numbers—on the move and the rights of people who cannot move. Both sets of people deserve attention, not only media but also ethical attention, and being granted the same rights postulated by the Universal Declaration of Human Rights, since they are as human as anybody else. Nujeen, now 21, is one of the "high profile supporters" featured on the website of the United Nations High Commissioner for Refugees and she collaborates with their online campaign to stand #WithRefugees (UNHCR 2018). Her commitment to human rights activism garners support on several platforms at once. This effort may be seen in her deployment of Twitter and its technological affordances, namely persistence, replicability, scalability, and searchability (boyd 2010), as well as "shareability" (Papacharissi 2012), thus amplifying the impact of what she narrates and disseminates. Indeed, Nujeen's collaboration across multiple platforms online and offline contributes to a sense of "co-construction" (Gilmore 2017) in her testimonial and self-narrating project that links her up with multiple other young women activists in contemporary times.

Notes

1. This is the narrator's preferred term for what others call Islamic State, IS, ISIL, or ISIS. She explains the reasons in her memoir (Mustafa and Lamb 2017, 94, 117).
2. See Martínez García (2019b).
3. Christina Lamb, Nujeen's coauthor, coauthor to another activist in this volume—Malala (see Chapter 2), works as a journalist for *The Sunday Times*.
4. See Martínez García (2017b, 2019c).

Works Cited

Alabed, Bana. 2017. *Dear World: A Syrian Girl's Story of War and Plea for Peace*. London: Simon & Schuster.

Barça Foundation. 2019. @FundacioFCB. *Twitter*. https://twitter.com/FundacioFCB. Accessed 23 January 2020.

BBC News. 2015a. Disabled Syrian Teenager's Journey Across Borders. *BBC*, 16 September. https://www.bbc.com/news/av/world-europe-34275165/disabled-syrian-teenager-s-journey-across-borders. Accessed 21 January 2020.

———. 2015b. Migrant Crisis: 'You should fight for what you want in this world'. *YouTube*, 17 September. https://www.youtube.com/watch?v=DwD3bosbDdQ. Accessed 23 January 2020.

———. 2018. BBC 100 Women 2018: Who Is on the List? *BBC*, 19 November. https://www.bbc.com/news/world-46225037. Accessed 23 January 2020.

Beverley, John. 1987. Anatomía del testimonio. *Revista de Crítica Literaria Latinoamericana* 25: 7–16.

boyd, danah. 2010. Social Network Sites as Networked Publics: Affordances, Dynamics, and Implications. In *A Networked Self: Identity, Community, and Culture on Social Network Sites*, ed. Zizi Papacharissi, 39–58. New York: Routledge.

Bruce, Mary. 2015. @marykbruce. *Twitter*, 17 September. https://twitter.com/marykbruce/status/644646987439173632. Accessed 21 January 2020.

Bruce, Mary, Dada Jovanovic, and Bartley Price. 2015. Soap Opera Stars Make Syrian Refugee's Dream Come True. *ABC News*, 28 September. https://abcnews.go.com/International/soap-opera-stars-make-syrian-refugees-dream-true/story?id=34111914. Accessed 23 January 2020.

Butler, Judith. 2004. *Precarious Life: The Powers of Mourning and Violence*. London: Verso.

———. 2005. Photography, War, Outrage. *PMLA* 120 (3): 822–827.

Douglas, Kate, and Anna Poletti. 2016. *Life Narratives and Youth Culture: Representation, Agency and Participation*. London: Palgrave Macmillan.

Genette, Gérard. 1997. *Paratexts: Thresholds of Interpretation*, trans. Jane E. Lewin. Cambridge: Cambridge University Press.

Gilmore, Leigh. 2017. Testimony. *a/b: Auto/Biography Studies* 32 (2): 307–309.

HarperCollins. 2019. William Collins. https://www.harpercollins.co.uk/corporate/harpercollins-imprints/william-collins/. Accessed 23 January 2020.

Hesford, Wendy S., and Wendy Kozol (eds.). 2005. *Just Advocacy?: Women's Human Rights, Transnational Feminisms, and the Politics of Representation*. New Brunswick, NJ: Rutgers University Press.

Human Rights Watch (HRW). 2019. Nujeen Mustafa, Syria. *Human Rights Watch*, 30 January. https://www.hrw.org/news/2019/01/31/nujeen-mustafa-syria. Accessed 23 January 2020.

Keen, Suzanne. 2008. Strategic Empathizing: Techniques of Bounded, Ambassadorial, and Broadcast Narrative Empathy. *Deutsche Vierteljahrsschrift für Literaturwissenchaft und Geistesgeschichte* 82 (3): 477–493.

Keen, Suzanne. 2016. Life Writing and the Empathetic Circle. *Concentric: Literary and Cultural Studies* 42 (2): 9–26.

Lamb, Christina. 2019. @christinalamb. *Twitter*, 15 February. https://twitter.com/christinalamb/status/1096339544478146560. Accessed 23 January 2020.

Last Week Tonight. 2015. Migrants and Refugees: Last Week Tonight with John Oliver (HBO). *YouTube*, 28 September. https://www.youtube.com/watch?v=umqvYhb3wf4. Accessed 13 March 2020.

Lee, Hyeonseo, and David John. 2015. *The Girl with Seven Names: A North Korean Defector's Story*. London: William Collins.

Lorraine, Sophia. 2017. *Bana Alabed: The Voice From Aleppo, Syria, That Moved the World: A Coloring Book Biography*. London: Gumdrop Press.

Mackey, Robert. 2015. Young Refugee Who Fled Syria in Wheelchair Thanks 'Days of Our Lives' Stars Who Reunited for Her. *New York Times*, 1 October. https://www.nytimes.com/2015/10/02/world/europe/young-refugee-who-fled-syria-in-wheelchair-thanks-days-of-our-lives-stars-who-reunited-for-her.html. Accessed 21 January 2020.

Martínez García, Ana Belén. 2017a. Unearthing the Past: Bringing Ideological Indoctrination to Light in North Korean Girls' Memoirs. *a/b: Auto/Biography Studies* 32 (3): 587–602.

———. 2017b. Bana Alabed: Using Twitter to Draw Attention to Human Rights Violations. *Prose Studies: History, Theory, Criticism* 39 (2–3): 132–149.

———. 2018. TED Talks as Life Writing: Online and Offline Activism. *Life Writing* 15 (4): 487–503.

———. 2019a. Construction and Collaboration in Life-Writing Projects: Malala Yousafzai's Activist 'I'. *Journal of Writing in Creative Practice* 12 (1–2): 201–217.

———. 2019b. Denouncing Human Trafficking in China: North Korean Women's Memoirs as Evidence. *State Crime Journal* 8 (1): 59–79.

———. 2019c. Empathy for Social Justice: The Case of Malala Yousafzai. *Journal of English Studies* 17: 253–275.

———. 2020. Women Activists' Strategies of Online Self-Presentation. *AI & Society: Journal of Knowledge, Culture and Communication*. Special Issue on Iteration as Persuasion in a Digital World. Forthcoming.

Mustafa, Nujeen. 2015. @NujeenMustafa. *Twitter*. https://twitter.com/nujeenmustafa. Accessed 23 January 2020.

———. 2017. I Am Not a Number: A Refugee's Tale. TEDxExeter. TEDxTalks. *YouTube*, 12 May. https://www.youtube.com/watch?v=R3r4gnSouqQ. Accessed 23 January 2020.

———. 2018. My Journey from Syria to Germany in a Wheelchair. TEDxNishtiman. TEDxTalks. *YouTube*, 28 August. https://www.youtube.com/watch?v=Y_Go10BibQ4. Accessed 23 January 2020.

Mustafa, Nujeen, and Christina Lamb. 2016. *Nujeen: One Girl's Incredible Journey from War-Torn Syria in a Wheelchair*. London: William Collins.

———. 2017. *The Girl from Aleppo: Nujeen's Escape from War to Freedom*. London: William Collins.

Office of the United Nations High Commissioner for Refugees (UNHCR). 2018. High Profile Supporters. https://www.unhcr.org/high-profile-supporters.html. Accessed 23 January 2020.

Oltermann, Philip. 2016. 'I hope Merkel Keeps Us': How Nujeen Mustafa Travelled from Syria to Germany in a Wheelchair. Interview. *The Guardian*,

19 September. https://www.theguardian.com/world/2016/sep/19/nujeen-mustafa-syria-isis-germany. Accessed 23 January 2020.
Papacharissi, Zizi. 2012. Without You, I'm Nothing: Performances of the Self on Twitter. *International Journal of Communication* 6: 1989–2006.
Patterson, Christina. 2016. Books: Nujeen: One Girl's Incredible Journey from War-torn Syria in a Wheelchair by Nujeen Mustafa with Christina Lamb. Review. *The Sunday Times*, 18 September. https://www.thetimes.co.uk/article/books-nujeen-one-girls-incredible-journey-from-war-torn-syria-in-a-wheelchair-by-nujeen-mustafa-with-christina-lamb-9j0lb5lxp. Accessed 23 January 2020.
Robin Show. 2015. Disabled Syrian Teenager's Journey Across Europe. *YouTube*, 24 September. https://www.youtube.com/watch?v=jg7KcXIbmAM. Accessed 23 January 2020.
Smith, Sidonie. 2006. Narratives and Rights: *Zlata's Diary* and the Circulation of Stories of Suffering Ethnicity. *WSQ: Women's Studies Quarterly* 34 (1–2): 133–152.
Smith, Sidonie, and Julia Watson. 2002. *Interfaces: Women, Autobiography, Image, Performance*. Ann Arbor: University of Michigan Press.
Whitlock, Gillian. 2007. *Soft Weapons: Autobiography in Transit*. Chicago: University of Chicago Press.
Worrall, Simon. 2016. This Girl Escaped From a Syrian War Zone in a Wheelchair. *National Geographic*, 6 November. https://www.nationalgeographic.com/news/2016/11/nujeen-mustafa-syria-wheelchair-christina-lamb/. Accessed 23 January 2020.

CHAPTER 7

Nadia Murad: Yazidi Survivor's Written vs Audiovisual Testimony

Abstract The final chapter closes as a coda to the first chapter in the book. If Malala Yousafzai received the Nobel Peace Prize in 2014, four years later, in 2018, it was Nadia Murad's turn. This chapter offers a similar approach to the one taken in the first chapter and elsewhere, which is to read the activist's texts side by side, and assess the narrative self-representation and self-construction processes in both written and audiovisual media, in traditional and innovative forms. Though there were prior memoirs by women who escaped ISIS recounting the horror of victimization and sexual exploitation, Murad's gained worldwide recognition faster perhaps aided by a multiplicity of other factors, namely the ubiquitous deployment of her life-writing texts—including a recent documentary—on and offline.

Keywords Nadia Murad · Yazidi survivor · Testimony · Victimization · Written/audiovisual · Online/offline

Nadia Murad was born in Kocho, Iraq, in 1993. Her parents were Yazidi, a minority whose religion is one of the oldest in the world. She was among the thousands of Yazidi women who were abducted, raped, and enslaved by self-proclaimed Islamic State in 2014. She also suffered the loss of six of her nine brothers and her mother. She became famous after having

A. B. Martínez García, *New Forms of Self-Narration*, Palgrave Studies in Life Writing, https://doi.org/10.1007/978-3-030-46420-2_7

escaped from slavery at the hands of ISIS and provided public testimony on behalf of her community.

Winning the Nobel Peace Prize

The final chapter closes as a coda to the first case study in the book (Chapter 2). If Malala Yousafzai received the Nobel Peace Prize in 2014, four years later it was the turn of Nadia Murad, Nobel Peace Prize recipient in 2018. The years elapsed in between have seen important advances in women's rights and minorities' rights, but also major related crises in many places across the globe. This chapter offers a similar approach to reading Nadia Murad's life writing as the one I have taken in this volume and elsewhere (see Martínez García 2019a), which is to read the activist's texts side by side, and assess the narrative self-representation and self-construction processes in both written and audiovisual media, looking at the "visual-verbal-virtual contexts" (Smith and Watson 2010, 167–192) that shape their life-writing project. Not only that, the similarities of these two women's life writing go deeper, as we account for their collaboration with renowned United Nations agencies, setting up their own nonprofit organization, and releasing a documentary a couple of years after publishing a memoir. In the case of Nadia Murad, a major actor is Amal Clooney, human rights lawyer and advocate, who has helped make her famous by providing her with a platform and access to politicians and legal counsel to demand accountability. In the case of Malala Yousafzai, no such figure can be elucidated at first glance. It would appear a lot of actors have played a role in erecting her as a public figure in the English-speaking world, for instance UK former PM Gordon Brown, US former President Barack Obama, and Canada's current President Justin Trudeau. However, none of those have made the long-standing commitment to Malala Yousafzai's cause that may be attributed to Amal Clooney in the case of Nadia Murad.

Sexual Slavery

If we consider a dizzying timeline of achievements, since 2014 when Murad managed to escape captivity and sex slavery, she has spoken out on many different occasions and at various venues for Yazidi girls held in captivity by Islamic State in Sinjar.[1] She was awarded refugee status in Germany, where she currently lives. There she set up social media profiles on Facebook (Murad 2015a) and Twitter (2015b), followed by speaking at the United Nations (2015c), founding Nadia's Initiative (2016a) and becoming Goodwill Ambassador for victims of violence (UNODC 2016), pledging to work toward a future where, as in the title of her memoir, she is "the last girl" to be raped, enslaved, and tortured (Murad 2017), being also awarded the Sakharov Prize (EU 2016) and the Nobel Peace Prize (Nobel 2018) among other public recognitions. The description of these traumatic events has been the focal point of her activism. In what follows, I trace some of the key components of her public discourse, who turned her from one Yazidi woman to a global icon for women's rights and ethnic or minority rights as human rights. Radically different from previous case studies in this book (Chapters 2–6), in major public speeches at international justice venues she relies on the help of an interpreter. It is, however, part of her strategy toward achieving empathy (Keen 2016). She would rather be regarded as an ethnic other than as an equal. It makes sense, then, that the chosen language be that of the minority. By refusing to speak in her broken English—which she could have well done—she is reasserting the value of her culture, the most vital of issues in her activism, since it is a culture on the verge of eradication. With the help of a translator, therefore, Nadia Murad testified at the 7585th meeting of the UN Security Council on 16 December 2015:

> rape was used to destroy women and girls, and to guarantee that these women could never live a normal life again … there were murders, collective slavery, and that needs to be qualified as genocide. I hope that you can convey this, the case of genocide, to the International Court. Please do this. (Murad 2015c)

In her UNODC Goodwill Ambassador acceptance speech, 16 September 2016, she further insisted on the idea of genocide (Murad 2016b):

> I'm most grateful to the UN Office on Drugs and Crime for appointing me Goodwill Ambassador for the Dignity of Survivors of Human Trafficking. I stand here today to represent those who are gone from us … This was genocide. It is that simple. In the matter of days, if not hours, thousands of Yazidis were killed and thousands of women and children were taken, just because they were Yazidis … I was used in the way they wanted to use me. I was not alone.

Importantly, Murad gives voice to the dead, in line with the duty of testimonial narratives (Smith and Watson 2012, 594), and to others who went through the same—a trait also shared with the other activists in this book. The witnessing "I" is a collective "I" in the transgressions it recalls and documents (600). The affirmation "I was not alone" (Murad 2016b) serves the purpose of authenticating the narrative—there may be further witnesses to what is recounted—and asserting a "communal identity" (Schaffer and Smith 2004, 134).

Coinciding with the 70th anniversary of the Universal Declaration of Human Rights, Nadia Murad spoke of the need to abolish modern-day slavery as enshrined in its Article 4 (OHCHR 2018). In her Nobel Peace Prize acceptance speech (Murad 2018), she stated her wish to represent silenced others:

> It's a great honour … to be a voice for those women who have been subjected to violence … I hope today marks the beginning of a new era, when peace is the priority and the world can collectively begin to define a new road map to protect women, children and minorities from persecution, in particular victims of sexual violence.

The voice of the victim-turned-survivor is symptomatic of what one has come to expect of testimonial texts. When the facts recounted are, moreover, of a sexual nature, there tend to be fewer first-hand witnesses who are willing to risk their honor by testifying to the wrongs committed against them. The stakes are high in giving witness. Women may be rejected by their communities, scorned, insulted, their testimony doubted (Gilmore 2017), themselves excluded and retraumatized by having to retell their experience.

Since its inception in September 2016, Nadia's Initiative (Murad 2016a) asserts its intention to expand beyond the local and advocate "globally for victims of violence":

> Nadia's Initiative challenges world leaders to act – to make "never again" a reality, not an empty promise. Words without action inflict the same harm and suffering as the perpetrators of mass atrocities and sexual violence.

Seeking the support of online and offline communities of women activists and advocates, Nadia's Initiative and Nadia Murad work hand in hand, in a similar way to how Malala Fund and Malala Yousafzai handle their accounts and awareness-raising campaigns. One person has become the face of the movement and of the organization, but multiple actors—most of them in the sidelines and anonymous—sustain a common objective. Murad's posts on Facebook (2015a) and Twitter (2015b) similarly collaborate with the shared aim of reaching disseminated audiences who, just from learning of Yazidis on one of those platforms, may turn to the other to fill in the gaps, again a recurrent strategy across the board for all the activists in this volume. Of interest is her online life writing handled in English, while not in the speeches mentioned earlier, which is a feature of her writing process also offline. The "never again" motto (Murad 2016a), linking up her activism with Holocaust memorialization (Kellner 1994), the #MeToo movement (Gilmore 2019), and the #NeverAgain gun control activists' campaign (Braun 2019), is affectively tied to the title of her memoir, *The Last Girl* (Murad 2017).

The Last Girl

The Last Girl (Murad 2017) has been published in two different forms—one prior to Murad's receiving the Nobel Peace Prize, one subsequent to the award. A memoir of a victim of sexual slavery, it is—like Yeonmi Park's (Chapter 4)—a "crude, hard-to-read testimonial" (Martínez García 2019b, 65), as readers empathize too strongly and may distance themselves from such a harrowing account. Its presence in best-selling lists worldwide and its being translated quickly into multiple languages, further proves its impact on international publics, though a note must be made that this is not the first such testimony to appear either in print or orally, as there were prior Yazidi girls speaking out of their captivity under Islamic State in Iraq (Shirin et al. 2016; Khalaf and Hoffmann 2016). Murad's memoir (Murad 2017) is set apart from those memoirs because it relies on existing templates for testimonial narratives such as the sex prisoner "ur-story" frame (Schaffer and Smith 2004, 140) far more heavily than they do. Here I provide a brief overview of some of the most outstanding rhetorical strategies that serve the purpose of making readers strategically empathize with the narrator-author and her cause.

English as a "rights lingua franca" is one of the strategies most common to young women activists' life-writing repertoire (Martínez García 2020). Contrary to Farida Khalaf's (Khalaf and Hoffmann 2016) and Shirin's et al. (2016) publishing their memoirs in German, Murad's (2017) is first printed in English. Though all three of them have been granted refugee status in Germany—which brings them close to Syrian activist Nujeen Mustafa (Chapter 6)—and Murad could have well decided to give her testimony in that language—given they are all made to study German upon relocation—, she chooses not to. To enter the public sphere, Murad makes the radical decision to rely on mediators that may help her reach a wider public by communicating her message in English. Following the example of multiple other activists before her, she chooses to provide testimony in her book with the help of this key mediation.[2]

Murad's (2017) memoir is framed as a testimony, and its claims are validated by a key mediator, a celebrity human rights barrister and advocate—Amal Clooney. Clooney is the person responsible for taking Murad's case before the UN Security Council. The foreword to the second edition, written by Clooney (ix–xi), serves as the perfect humanitarian frame to the text. Clooney emphasizes certain vital ideas underlying human rights discourse, for instance "voice" (Schaffer and Smith 2004, 74). Even if, for an informed reader, this foreword is unnecessary, it evinces a clear editorial strategy, since it could have been either obviated or inserted as a blurb on front or back cover. Clooney's impassioned defense of Nadia Murad's "voice" opens the door to reading this memoir as a testimony. On the page, Clooney's words remind readers of a defense attorney's closing speech before the court, hammering out a rhythmic short text full of "strategic nuanced repetition" (Martínez García 2019a, 212) that will stay in their minds:

> Over the time I have known her, Nadia has not only found her *voice*, she has become the *voice* of every Yazidi who is a victim of genocide, every woman who has been abused, every refugee who has been left behind.
>
> Those who thought that by their cruelty they could silence her were wrong. Nadia Murad's spirit is not broken, and her *voice* will not be muted. Instead, through this book, her *voice* is louder than ever. (Clooney 2017, xi; emphasis added)

The close repetition of "voice" throughout this short passage sets the stage for what follows—in this case, the full body of the text, comprising Murad's (2017) testimony. It is an invitation to read the "I" of the memoir as Nadia Murad's, and to engage emotionally and ethically with the experiences contained therein.

Murad's testimonial stance, like other activist life-writers', deploys pronouns strategically (see Martínez García 2019c). The "I" and the "we" are in constant negotiation. Thus, the first chapter opens with a description of the oddity of her opinions and actions as she was growing up, with a young Nadia rebelling against what most of the tribe thought was normal, like letting a shepherd be taken by ISIS: "I was outspoken and I wanted to be heard, and I felt giant in my anger" (Murad 2017, 10). But even her mother disapproved of her behavior: "It's shameful for you to do that, Nadia, it's not your business" (Murad 2017, 12). The first chapter thus contributes to a sort of feminist self-representation.

The following chapter, however, marks a departure from the first-person singular toward the first-person plural, embracing her roots and celebrating Yazidism. Murad adopts the plural pronoun to emphasize her belonging to a community. In so doing, both the "I" and the "we" become collective (Martínez García 2017, 588). Murad resorts to this strategy throughout her memoir, as well as in her public appearances, particularly when she wants to highlight how Yazidis have been—and still are—misunderstood, maltreated, harassed, persecuted, and so on. For example, she recounts the external pressures coming from all sides to make Yazidis conform to an identity imposed—and constructed for geopolitical purposes—by others:

> A lot of people complained privately that the KDP pressured them into supporting the party and into saying Yazidis were Kurds and Sinjar was part of Kurdistan. Iraqi politicians ignored us, and Saddam had tried to force *us* to say *we* were Arab,[3] as though *we* could all be threatened into giving up *our* identities and that once we did *we* would never rebel. (Murad 2017, 21; emphasis added)

Another interesting example showcasing the pronoun-shift strategy is when Murad mentions the role of Saddam in the aftermath of the Gulf War a little further on:

> *I* was born just two years after the first Gulf War and five years after the Iran-Iraq War, a pointless eight-year conflict that seemed to fulfill Saddam's desire to torture his people more than anything else. The memories of these children, who *we* would never see again, lived like ghosts in our house. (23; emphasis added)

The narrating "I" resorts to moving from the first-person singular to the plural pronoun, even if she was only a child at the time and could therefore not have witnessed the events she so pointedly denounces. This calls to mind polemic cases such as Rigoberta Menchú's (1984) *testimonio*, or North Korean activists' testimonial life-writing projects (Martínez García 2019b, 74; see Chapters 3 and 4).

Apart from discussing Saddam's authoritarian regime and grip on power, the narrating "I" inscribes herself in History by explaining what followed the Gulf War, the American invasion of Iraq and the formation of a new Kurdistan (Murad 2017, 36–45).

When Murad describes the plight of the displaced by Islamic State, she does so in thorough detail, as if she had been there. Though problematic because the narrator was not there to be as certain as she sounds, she chooses minute—and emotional—description to shed light on gross injustice and "to maximize the affective load of the passage" (Martínez García 2017, 591):

> As the Yazidis walked toward the mountain, they dropped much of what they carried ... Children dragged their feet until their shoes split apart beneath them. When they reached the mountain, some scrambled straight up the craggy sides while others hid in caves, temples, or mountain villages. Cars sped along the winding roads, some tumbling over the sides when the drivers, in their haste, lost control. The mountain's plateaus became crowded with the displaced. (Murad 2017, 58–59)

Read under the lens of testimony, the quote reveals a truth that lack of witnesses might render invisible (Felman 1992, 210). This is just but one instance where the testifying agent makes readers secondary witnesses to the trauma of a community of oppressed others. Murad makes a political statement when faced with silenced parts of the history of the collective of afflicted individuals to which she belongs.

One of the most harrowing parts of the memoir is when she describes the irreparable damage her family endured at the hands of ISIS. Murad combines second-hand testimony—things she heard or was told—with first-hand testimony—what she herself saw. In recounting the killing of two of her brothers, the "eye-witness" (Smith and Watson 2012, 590) as "I-witness" (609) makes a strong appeal to readers to witness to her and her family's suffering which somehow reminds readers of Menchú's (1984) recounting of the horror of her brother's murder (201–211):

> I scanned the trucks and the garden, searching for my brothers. *I saw* Massoud standing in the second truck, staring straight ahead along with

> the other men, avoiding looking up at the crowded window or back at the village ...
>
> Next *I saw* Elias, walking slowly in line toward the same truck. The man who had been a father to all of us after our own father died looked completely defeated ... *I couldn't turn away*. Everything around me faded–the noise of the women weeping, the militants' heavy footsteps, the harsh afternoon sun, even the heat seemed to disappear as *I watched* my brothers being loaded onto the trucks, Massoud in the corner and Elias in the back. Then the doors closed, and the trucks drove away to behind the school. A moment later *we heard* gunshots.
>
> I fell away from the window as the room erupted in screams ...
>
> I prayed that my mother hadn't *seen* her sons loaded onto the trucks, as *I had*. (Murad 2017, 102–103; emphasis added)

The previous passage serves as an introduction to the endless list of atrocities Murad denounces in her memoir. Each human rights violation is described in detail to effect the necessary "empathic unsettlement" (LaCapra 2001, 102) and depends on the "strategic use of emotions" (Martínez García 2017, 598)—the trademark of all the human rights life-writing projects contained in the present book. Reliving the pain is necessary if the activist-narrator is to raise awareness of injustices committed against her, her family, and her community.

Among the most deeply felt losses, is the loss of her mother: "My mother was on one of the last trucks. I'll never forget how she looked" (Murad 2017, 111). This willingness to remember, despite the pain, strikes an "emotional chord" (Martínez García 2018, 497) in readers, as the narrator goes on to describe the way she looked that day, in that precise moment. The urgency of memory, of recalling every single detail that might bring her mother closer back to life, is in extreme tension with the passing of time and an inner battle between calling forth and suppressing painful memories. This conflict between the will to forget and "the obligation to remember" (Volf 2006, 205) is expressed in Chapter 11 of Part II, when Murad recalls the humiliation experienced while being raped and abused by key actors in the process. That she chooses to repeat their names and what they did, as well as the words "I remember" and "I will never forget" (Murad 2017, 185) is crucial, as she is not reliving the trauma to excite pity, but to advocate for justice.

In Chapter 8 of Part I, mourning rituals are described (Murad 79–81). A pronounced sense of collective identification is the reason for such detail. It is placed strategically right before ISIS enters and controls the village, and it foreshadows what they will do. Far more destructive, in psychological terms, than the physical injuries of being maimed, abducted, raped, or killed, is the fact that bodies will be left unburied and unmourned (Murad 2017, 81). The narrating "I" testifies to what she and other Yazidis view as a crime against humanity—the basic human right to mourn one's people with the appropriate rites. The narrator's remembering the dead is a tribute to those who died unclaimed, "ungrieved" (Butler 2009, 74). Not only are the dead mourned, but so is the home that is lost. The "I" describes the scene the last time she saw her home in an emotional manner, adding details that appeal to all senses, vividly depicting smells, sounds, views (Murad 2017, 90), thus connecting loss and nostalgia.

As in the case of Malala, with whom I started this book (Chapter 2), "the rhetorical emphatic repetition of certain phrases is noteworthy" (Martínez García 2019a, 204). Emphatic repetition is used to convey emotions and thus to actively construe empathic engagements between the narrator and the reader (Martínez García 2019c, 261). As the narrating "I" relays all the terrible things about ISIS "I didn't know" (Murad 2017, 94), the reader is warned of horrors to come in the ensuing pages. Similarly, rhetorical questions function, here as in other memoirs (see Filipović 1995; Yousafzai and Lamb 2013), as ethical calls for attention (Smith 2006, 148): "why wasn't anyone helping us? … Why hadn't anyone helped us?" (Murad 2017, 110). These questions—with their nuanced repetition of "why"—go unanswered, like Malala's rhetorical "why's" (Martínez García 2019c, 268), forcing readers to bear witness to the trauma.

In clear correlation to Yeonmi Park's (2015) memoir of human trafficking (Chapter 4), Nadia Murad's (2017) memoir makes strong appeals against the dehumanizing practices at the heart of trafficking.[4] Both Yeonmi Park's and Nadia Murad's descriptions of the atrocities they endured confront readers with "emotional, often overwhelming, accounts of dehumanization, brutal and violent physical harm, and exploitation" (Smith and Watson 2010, 133). In the latter memoir, the narrating "I" therefore insists on how Yazidis were treated as animals, as not just inferior but subhuman beings, or even as objects. This issue must be consistently emphasized in the memoir, since it is the core of Nadia Murad's activism. Here I will just comment on some examples representative of the condemning voice that can be heard throughout.

When Murad and other Yazidi girls are abducted from Kocho by ISIS, they are pushed inside crammed buses that quickly become symbolic for Holocaust transport, trucks carrying inmates to prison, or animals to the slaughterhouse:

> The bus was huge, with at least forty rows of six seats cut down the middle by a long lit aisle and surrounded by windows that were covered by drawn curtains. As the seats filled, the air quickly became heavy and hard to breathe, but when we tried to open the windows, or even the curtains so that we could see outside, a militant yelled at us to sit still. (Murad 2017, 117–118)

Moreover, something in the disquieting description recalls the Middle Passage, perhaps a strategy on the part of the narrating "I" to embed her testimony within the larger framework of rights discourse by harking back at representations of the slave trade and the long-standing tradition of slave narratives, both Transatlantic, American, or of "harem literature" (Whitlock 2007, 100). Murad is also brutalized, treated as less than human, and the physical conditions of the transport are not fit for any person (Murad 2017, 118). Being enslaved is the next step that brings Murad's testimony closer to the Middle Passage ones: "We were no longer human beings–we were sabaya" (123). "Sabaya" is the plural form of the Arabic word "sabiyya," which though commonly translated as "young girl" was used as a dehumanizing label by ISIS fighters to refer to the "young women they would buy and sell as sex slaves" (122).

Though the abuse endured on the first day of her abduction may seem innocuous to some, it has a toll on Murad's psyche. At 21, she was still a virgin, in a deeply religious family and traditional community that always taught her she should be a virgin until marriage:

> I closed my eyes again, praying that he would go away, and then I felt his hand move slowly across my shoulder, brushing my neck, and then down the front of my dress until it stopped over my left breast. It felt like fire; I had never been touched like that before. I opened my eyes but didn't look at him, I just looked straight ahead. Abu Batat reached inside my dress and grabbed my breast, hard as if he wanted to hurt me, and then walked away. (119)

This brutal groping marks the start of a mental decline which consequences Murad carries to this day: "Every second with ISIS was part of a slow, painful death–of the body and the soul–and that moment on the bus with Abu Batat was the moment I started dying" (119). The torture endured at the hands of ISIS is as much physical as it is psychological. After being bought, she recalls, "my body hurt and went numb wherever Hajji Salman's fingers went" (147). But, far more damaging to her psyche, it seems, is being forced to marry—"With these 'marriages'[5] ISIS continued their slow murder of Yazidi girls" (151)—and convert, for "Who was I if I wasn't Yazidi?" (151). Feeling "empty" (151), hollow, or numb, reappears throughout the memoir, emphasizing a progressive dissociation that is a recurrent feature in rape testimonies, as it is one of the many symptoms of post-traumatic stress disorder or PTSD (American Psychiatric Association [APA] 1994, 424–425).[6] In order to avoid the pain, a coping strategy is to go through the motions in mechanical fashion: "Your body doesn't belong to you … There is only rape and the numbness that comes with accepting that this is now your life" (Murad 2017, 186). Losing one's rights over one's body, as I have commented when discussing Yeonmi Park's (Chapter 4) memories of human trafficking (Martínez García 2019b, 65), is among the most traumatic realizations. Dissociation, mentioned above, becomes increasingly more marked, so much so that in the extract just quoted the pronoun chosen is "you," as if addressing the self from the outside. This extract, in turn, closely correlates to Yeonmi Park's out-of-body experience (2015, 146), discussed in Martínez García (2019b, 70).

In the slave market in Mosul, Murad describes the trauma of being objectified, dehumanized:[7]

> It was like the scene of an explosion. We moaned as though wounded, doubling over and vomiting on the floor, but none of it stopped the militants …
>
> They gravitated toward the most beautiful girls first, asking, "How old are you?" and examining their hair and mouths. "They are virgins, right?" they asked a guard, who nodded and said, "Of course!" like a shopkeeper taking pride in his product … Now the militants touched us anywhere they wanted, running their hands over our breasts and our legs, as if we were animals. (Murad 2017, 136–137)

Murad repeats her critique of the dehumanization of being sold when she details the reasons why there might be something worse than being turned into a slave—the cyclic nature of the process:

> Being bought once as a slave, having your humanity and dignity taken from you, was bad enough, and I couldn't stand the thought of being passed from militant to militant, moved from house to house, and maybe even transported across the border into ISIS-held Syria, like an object at the market, like a sack of flour in the back of a truck. (177)

Beyond the pain of being treated "as if we were animals" (137), lies feeling "like an object at the market" (177). Murad repeats the idea that they all die a slow death, and compares it to how Yazidi men, by being executed, did not suffer quite as much as the women did: "Being dead was better than being sold like merchandise and raped until our bodies were in shreds ... When you are a sabiyya, you die every second of every day" (182). The accumulated pain that never ends creates a sense of anxious gloominess, more poignantly so if all the children and women still unaccounted for are taken into consideration. The picture Murad's testimony is painting serves an even higher purpose, relating not just to the suffering endured by Yazidis, but expanding it to encompass the "unspoken narratives of other victims of the same rights violation" (Smith and Watson 2012, 594).

Murad's recollection of being raped, central to her activism as a spokesperson for Yazidi girl survivors of sexual slavery by ISIS, gives voice to other victims:

> Over the past three years, I have heard a lot of stories about other Yazidi women who were captured and enslaved by ISIS. For the most part, we were all victims of the same violence. We would be *bought* at the market, *or given* as a gift ... we would be *raped and* humiliated, most of us *beaten* as well. Then we would be *sold or given* as a gift again, and again *raped and beaten*, then *sold or given* to another militant, and *raped and beaten* by him, and *sold or given*, and *raped and beaten*, and it went this way for as long as we were desirable enough and not yet dead. (Murad 2017, 161; emphasis added)

Thus, Murad denounces the crimes committed against them, herself included, adopting the collective stance typical of testimony (Hesford 2004, 105). Instead of describing the rape in detail, she chooses to collectivize her plight. The repetitive nature of her testimony is a rhetorical strategy in so far as it creates an atmosphere of absolute despair and lack of hope. A cyclic pattern of rape, abuse, and dehumanization, tantamount to torture and to the degradation of the human subject, seems inescapable and is meant to foster emotional engagement—or engagement in "affective transactions" (Whitlock 2015, 68), and, beyond emotions, ethical engagement.

Switching back to the "I" Murad explains why she does not want to focus solely on her personal experience. On the one hand, and in a rather confessional tone, she admits to the fact that she was never capable of fighting back: "I have never admitted this to anyone, but I did not fight back when Hajji Salman or anyone else came to rape me" (2017, 162). On the other hand, it is her way of fighting ISIS back and reclaiming the humanity she had been stripped of. Reminiscing how she thought "I am not brave" (162) and how "I felt so alone that I barely felt human" (163), the narrating "I" is now telling her story to the world, thus being brave and uniting herself with all the other victims. By refusing to be silent any longer, she defies ISIS's willingness to subdue and possess them, to commoditize, dehumanize, and exterminate them.

Unexpectedly, the rape is recreated at the end of the chapter (165–166). Instead of urging readers to empathize by means of detailed descriptions as was the case of Shirin's et al. (2016) and Farida's (Khalaf and Hoffmann 2016) narratives, what Murad does is to poetically recreate in her mind the whole scene, with enough room for the reader's imagination to do the rest:

> Each moment was terrifying. If I pulled away, he roughly pulled me back. He was loud enough for the guard to hear–he shouted as if he wanted all of Mosul to know that he was finally raping his sabiyya–and no one interfered. His touch was exaggerated, forceful, meant to hurt me. No man ever touched his wife like this. Hajji Salman was as big as a house, as big as the house we were in. And I was like a child, crying out for my mother. (Murad 2017, 166)

Readers are meant to feel outrage. Murad was 21 when this occurred, but her being a virgin, skinny, and tiny, immediately calls forth the image of the child of humanitarian narratives in need of protection that has lost it all.

A notable point of coincidence between this memoir (Murad 2017) and Malala's (Yousafzai and Lamb 2013) is how the narrating "I" reclaims her identity by reinstating her first name once she manages to escape from the grasp of the terrorists and wishes to become an activist (Martínez García 2019a, 206). In Nadia's case, the phrase is further accompanied of a vital piece of information that she needs in order to reconstruct who she is. Hence, she presents herself as "My name is Nadia ... I am a Yazidi" (Murad 2017, 209) and "I'm Nadia ... I'm a Yazidi" (260). Ever since her escape from ISIS, her first name—her individual self—is as important as her "plural 'I'" (Hesford 2004, 124). The individual and the collective are deeply enmeshed and cannot be separated. Nadia refuses to be constrained by those who might argue she had converted to Islam and was therefore no longer a Yazidi. Her refusal is part of her claiming agency back from the abusers. Very much like Malala (Chapter 2), Nadia's decision to speak out is rooted in the belief that life writing may be harnessed for sociopolitical purposes and actual change (Martínez García 2019c). However, Nadia is far more aware of the risks she may incur, not only to her personal safety, but to becoming subsumed in other people's vested interests:

> I was quickly learning that my story, which I still thought of as a personal tragedy, could be someone else's political tool, particularly in a place like Iraq. I would have to be careful what I said, because words mean different things to different people, and your story can easily become a weapon to be turned on you. (Murad 2017, 265)

After having suffered so much at the hands of ISIS, partly due to the lack of help that the Yazidi community received from its neighbors, Nadia is not ready to comply to their version of the events now. This early realization of the political stakes attached to her testimony, far from silencing her, made her a more conscious speaker and spokesperson for the cause.

Auto/Biographical Documentary

One of Nadia Murad's latest life-writing texts is the auto/biographical documentary *On Her Shoulders* (Bombach 2018). Contrary to what one may learn of her life if one reads her memoir, this documentary is geared at garnering support for her cause without retelling her story. Attention, therefore, should be paid to her silences and how they call for redress. The documentary succeeds in ways Malala Yousafzai's (Guggenheim 2015) did not, engaging the audience by refusing to give morbid details. Its goal is to make viewers see what Nadia's current life is, not what it was. It also shows how life for other Yazidis is like now. Thus, her current activist campaigning for justice for the Yazidi as well as for victims of sexual violence is understood under a different lens—radical ethical distance. If interested in knowing more of the context, viewers can turn to online and offline material, but no explicit mention of either is made.

On Her Shoulders (Bombach 2018) was released in the United States on 19 October 2018, in the UK on 25 January 2019. Directed by Alexandria Bombach, it has received 11 awards and been nominated to multiple other awards, mostly related to human rights documentaries, but not only in that field. The documentary paints a vivid picture of who Nadia is, but without turning her into a celebrity as it happened in Malala's case with *He Named Me Malala* (Guggenheim 2015). There are further differences worth noting.

The filmmaker does not appear on screen, not even as a voiceover or a presence sensed off camera. This is vital for the empathetic engagement of the audience with Nadia, the absolute protagonist of the story: It strategically presents Nadia's actions and words as unmediated testimony. Bombach (2018) manages to cut across the ethnic/cultural/social divide by focusing on everyday life, thus exemplifying what Suzanne Keen might call authorial "broadcast strategic narrative empathy" (2016, 22)—spectators share some experiences with these Yazidi people on screen, like the intimate, mundane scenes of home cooking. Bombach (2018) also deploys "ambassadorial" (Keen 2016, 20) techniques of empathy: She forces viewers to look from the outside on the lives of Yazidis, particularly when Nadia is visiting them in refugee camps, in Turkey and Greece, and giving rallies for relocated communities in Germany and Canada. They live in appalling conditions, which, as many other documentaries on refugees have done, poses an ethical dilemma (on appropriating the pain/suffering/trauma/life of others) and resorts to commonplaces like the need for the activist (in this case, Nadia) to stand for the oppressed.

If we compare Nadia's documentary (Bombach 2018) to Malala's documentary (Guggenheim 2015), some coincidences come to light, for instance its presentation at Sundance and the fact that the release was pushed back until after the Nobel Peace Prize had been awarded. However, while Guggenheim (2015) chose to wait until then for a last-minute addition of what happened and then changed the whole film so it would become a retrospective narrative leading up to the moment Malala won, this is not what matters for Bombach (2018). Nadia is not even featured in the title. Her name does not matter: that is why her responses in interviews are not shown here. Rather, what matters is the collective suffering. A "collective identity" (Hesford 2004, 128) is presented by focusing on many different people across her travels. This is a tribute to her people, the Yazidis, men and women and children, "whose voice is not heard" (Bombach 2018), an aim which is actually expressed in much the same way by other people on screen. They need her to continue to speak out. Either because of shame or because she is like a "beacon of hope" (SDG 2019), they need her to continue to do her advocacy work. She is shown doubting and wishing to stop at times, but those around her convince her she is needed and must not stop. For Nadia, what is "on her shoulders" is this massive weight of responsibility: She would like to step out of the limelight, not to speak of the horrible past, perhaps to forget as many trauma victims avow, but she cannot because her moral duty is to carry on the fight for justice on behalf of her people. Spectators' duty, the auto/biographical documentary apparently suggests, is to be witnesses to this (individual and) collective plight (Hesford 2004, 106).

First-Person Witnessing and Empathy

Attending to the ways first-person testimony of sexual violence is linked up in human rights claims has been discussed by Leigh Gilmore (2017) as geared at eliciting empathy but subject to the latter failing and raising doubts regarding the witness's credibility (130–131).

There are differences and similarities between Nadia's testimony of rape—both her own and other Yazidi girls' and women's—and that of other Yazidi survivors who also published their memoirs but who chose to do so first in German (Shirin et al. 2016; Khalaf and Hoffmann 2016), which dramatically reduced the impact they would eventually have on the global market and public sphere. Both Shirin and Farida Khalaf chose to present themselves as innocent victims of rape and genocide, their stories calling for pity and intent on presenting a story of dramatic—and traumatic—events. They did so by claiming the personal injuries they sustained, describing in gory detail the torture they endured at the hands of ISIS, and their memoirs are consequently read more as the memoirs of survivors of rape than as testimonies. They seek the same goal as Nadia's—bringing public attention to the victimization of Yazidis and calling for justice—but the ways they try to reach this goal are quite dissimilar. Instead of adopting the first-person plural stance, as Nadia does throughout the memoir, they employ the singularity of their personal trauma. This is not detrimental to making readers/audience care. However, they have not managed to harness the popular appeal Nadia has. They have admittedly entered the arena of those icons who the public refers to on a first-name basis. But they have not been called to testify as many times as she has, nor have they received so many humanitarian awards. One can only guess what is at stake. All these survivors are living in Germany, all of them sought refuge there after leaving Iraq and the refugee camp behind, all had to learn German. But only Nadia was approached by an activist seeking a voice that might represent their plight in the UK (Murad 2017, 268–269). Perhaps her older age and rage, her willingness to speak out, made her stand out. As in Malala's case, Nadia may not have been the first option. One may never know if more girls were offered the same role. What is important is that she agreed to become this person, this spokesperson for the cause of Yazidis, this persona who would lead a public life without so much as a remnant of a past where she had a private life.

Notes

1. As opposed to Nujeen Mustafa (Chapter 6), who refuses to call them by any other term than Daesh, Nadia Murad (2017) chooses Islamic State, which is omnipresent, right from the title of her memoir.
2. For more on mediation of testimonial narratives entering the public sphere, see Martínez García 2021.
3. See Chapter 6 in this volume for how Nujeen Mustafa similarly denounces how her Kurdish identity is being subsumed by the authorities into the larger and wrongly-assumed-to-be Arab identity.
4. See also Chapter 6 for Nujeen Mustafa's criticism of the dehumanization endured by trafficking victims, though not subject to sexual violence.
5. For a discussion of forced marriage contravening the Convention on the Elimination of All Forms of Discrimination against Women (CEDAW) (OHCHR 1979), see Martínez García (2019b, 68).
6. This identity crisis further reminds readers of North Korean memoirs, when they struggle to come to terms with being trafficked (Martínez García 2019b).
7. See Martínez García (2019b) for similar experiences of North Korean women sold in China.

Works Cited

American Psychiatric Association (APA). 1994. *Diagnostic and Statistical Manual of Mental Health Disorders*, 4th ed and rev. ed. Washington, DC: American Psychiatric Association.

Bombach, Alexandria. 2018. *On Her Shoulders*. USA: RYOT Films.

Braun, Eric. 2019. *Never Again: The Parkland Shooting and the Teen Activists Leading a Movement*. Minneapolis: Lerner.

Butler, Judith. 2009. *Frames of War: When Is Life Grievable?* London: Verso.

Clooney, Amal. 2017. Foreword. In *The Last Girl: My Story of Captivity and My Fight Against the Islamic State*, ix–xi. London: Virago.

EU Affairs. 2016. Sakharov Prize: Nadia Murad and Lamiya Aji Bashar to Receive This Year's Award. *European Parliament News*, 8 December. https://www.europarl.europa.eu/news/en/headlines/eu-affairs/20161202STO54446/sakharov-prize-nadia-murad-and-lamiya-aji-bashar-to-receive-this-year-s-award. Accessed 2 March 2020.

Felman, Shoshana. 1992. The Return of the Voice: Claude Lanzmann's *Shoah*. In *Testimony: Crises of Witnessing in Literature, Psychoanalysis, and History*, ed. S. Felman and D. Laub, 204–283. New York: Routledge.

Filipović, Zlata. 1995. *Zlata's Diary: A Child's Life in Sarajevo*, trans. Christina Pribichevich-Zoric. London: Penguin.

Gilmore, Leigh. 2017. *Tainted Witness: Why We Doubt What Women Say About Their Lives*. New York: Columbia University Press.

———. 2019. Frames of Witness: The Kavanaugh Hearings, Survivor Testimony, and #MeToo. *Biography* 42 (3): 610–623.

Guggenheim, Davis. 2015. *He Named Me Malala*. United Arab Emirates: Image Nation Abu Dhabi.

Hesford, Wendy S. 2004. Documenting Violations: Rhetorical Witnessing and the Spectacle of Distant Suffering. *Biography* 27 (1): 104–144.

Keen, Suzanne. 2016. Life Writing and the Empathetic Circle. *Concentric: Literary and Cultural Studies* 42 (2): 9–26.

Kellner, Hans. 1994. "Never Again" Is Now. *History and Theory* 33 (2): 127–144.

Khalaf, Farida, and Andrea C. Hoffmann. 2016. *The Girl Who Beat ISIS: Farida's Story*, trans. Jamie Bulloch. London: Square Peg.

LaCapra, Dominick. 2001. *Writing History, Writing Trauma*. Baltimore: Johns Hopkins University Press.

Martínez García, Ana Belén. 2017. Unearthing the Past: Bringing Ideological Indoctrination to Light in North Korean Girls' Memoirs. *a/b: Auto/Biography Studies* 32 (3): 587–602.

———. 2018. TED Talks as Life Writing: Online and Offline Activism. *Life Writing* 15 (4): 487–503.

———. 2019a. Construction and Collaboration in Life-Writing Projects: Malala Yousafzai's Activist 'I'. *Journal of Writing in Creative Practice* 12 (1–2): 201–217.

———. 2019b. Denouncing Human Trafficking in China: North Korean Women's Memoirs as Evidence. *State Crime Journal* 8 (1): 59–79.

———. 2019c. Empathy for Social Justice: The Case of Malala Yousafzai. *Journal of English Studies* 17: 253–275.

———. 2020. Women Activists' Strategies of Online Self-Presentation. *AI & Society: Journal of Knowledge, Culture and Communication*. Special Issue on Iteration as Persuasion in a Digital World. Forthcoming.

———. 2021. Refugees' Mediated Narratives in the Public Sphere. *Narrative*. Special Issue on Narrative in the Public Sphere. Forthcoming.

Menchú, Rigoberta. 1984. *I, Rigoberta Menchú: An Indian Woman in Guatemala*, ed. Elisabeth Burgos-Debray and trans. Ann Wright. London: Verso.

Murad, Nadia. 2015a. @NadiaMuradBasee. *Facebook*. https://www.facebook.com/NadiaMuradBasee/. Accessed 2 March 2020.

———. 2015b. @NadiaMuradBasee. *Twitter*. https://twitter.com/nadiamuradbasee. Accessed 2 March 2020.

———. 2015c. Nadia Murad Basee Taha (ISIL victim) on Trafficking of Persons in Situations of Conflict—Security Council, 7585th Meeting. *UN Web TV*, 16 December. http://webtv.un.org/meetings-events/watch/nadia-murad-basee-taha-isil-victim-on-trafficking-of-persons-in-situations-of-conflict-security-council-7585th-meeting/4665835954001. Accessed 2 March 2020.

———. 2016a. *Nadia's Initiative*. https://nadiasinitiative.org/. Accessed 2 March 2020.

———. 2016b. Speech on Her Appointment as UN Goodwill Ambassador, 16 September 2016. *YouTube*. https://www.youtube.com/watch?v=1SKDgnUTZLA. Accessed 2 March 2020.

———. 2017. *The Last Girl: My Story of Captivity and My Fight Against the Islamic State*. London: Virago.

———. 2018. Nadia Murad: Nobel Peace Prize lecture 2018 (English subtitles). *YouTube*, 10 December. https://www.youtube.com/watch?v=CqB0cMvGnIk. Accessed 3 March 2020.

Nobel Prize. 2018. The Nobel Peace Prize for 2018. *The Nobel Prize*, 5 October. https://www.nobelprize.org/prizes/peace/2018/press-release/. Accessed 2 March 2020.

Office of the High Commissioner for Human Rights (OHCHR). 1979. Convention on the Elimination of All Forms of Discrimination against Women. http://www.ohchr.org/Documents/ProfessionalInterest/cedaw.pdf. Accessed 4 March 2020.

———. 2018. Universal Declaration of Human Rights at 70: 30 Articles on 30 Articles—Article 4. *OHCHR News*, 10 December. https://www.ohchr.org/EN/NewsEvents/Pages/DisplayNews.aspx?NewsID=23866&LangID=E. Accessed 3 March 2020.

Park, Yeonmi. 2015. *In Order to Live: A North Korean Girl's Journey to Freedom*. London: Penguin.

Schaffer, Kay, and Sidonie Smith. 2004. *Human Rights and Narrated Lives: The Ethics of Recognition*. New York: Palgrave.

Shirin, Alexandra Cavelius, and Jan Kizilhan. 2016. *Ich bleibe eine Tochter des Lichts: Meine Flucht aus den Fängen der IS-Terroristen*. Berlin: Europa Verlag.

Smith, Sidonie. 2006. Narratives and Rights: *Zlata's Diary* and the Circulation of Stories of Suffering Ethnicity. *WSQ: Women's Studies Quarterly* 34 (1–2): 133–152.

Smith, Sidonie, and Julia Watson. 2010. *Reading Autobiography: A Guide for Interpreting Life Narratives*, 2nd ed. Minneapolis: Minnesota University Press.

———. 2012. Witness or False Witness?: Metrics of Authenticity, Collective I-Formations, and the Ethic of Verification in First-Person Testimony. *Biography* 35 (4): 590–626.

Sustainable Development Goals Advocates (SDG Advocates). 2019. Nadia Murad. https://www.unsdgadvocates.org/news/nadia-murad. Accessed 4 March 2020.

United Nations Office on Drugs and Crime (UNODC). 2016. Human Trafficking Survivor Nadia Murad Named UNODC Goodwill Ambassador. *UNODC*, 16 September. https://www.unodc.org/unodc/en/frontpage/2016/September/human-trafficking-survivor-nadia-murad-named-unodc-goodwill-ambassador.html. Accessed 2 March 2020.

Volf, Miroslav. 2006. *The End of Memory: Remembering Rightly in a Violent World*. Grand Rapids, MI: Wm. B. Eerdmans.

Whitlock, Gillian. 2007. *Soft Weapons: Autobiography in Transit*. Chicago: University of Chicago Press.

———. 2015. *Postcolonial Life Narratives: Testimonial Transactions*. Oxford: Oxford University Press.

Yousafzai, Malala, and Christina Lamb. 2013. *I Am Malala: The Girl Who Stood Up for Education and Was Shot by the Taliban*. London: Weidenfeld & Nicolson.

CHAPTER 8

Conclusion: Victim Girls Becoming Activist Women

Abstract This book reveals the ways in which young women resort to social media as well as traditional media as part of their ongoing life-writing project. The phenomenon of virality is explored to cast light on the affordances that facilitate synergies among significant social and political actors on the global stage. It does not offer a completely positive view of the digital, but states the possibilities that the combination of online and offline methods offers and opens the door to future explorations in novel forms of narrating the self. *New Forms of Self-Narration* addresses the strategic use of names, labeling and tagging. Each chapter underscores the multiplicity of approaches to life writing and mediation these young women activists take, showcasing relevant trends in twenty-first-century life writing.

Keywords Ongoing · Viral phenomena · Global · Mediation · Young women activists · Contemporary life writing

Viral Phenomena, Ephemeral Fads?

Going viral online creates ripples offline. Conversely, a shocking life story offline may reverberate online. These performances, on and offline, are like "life vignettes" (Martínez García 2018, 498) to be assembled by witnessing readers/audiences and which, taken together, exemplify life

A. B. Martínez García, *New Forms of Self-Narration*, Palgrave Studies in Life Writing, https://doi.org/10.1007/978-3-030-46420-2_8

writing in the making. This book has sought to reveal the ways in which young women resort to social media as well as traditional media as part of their ongoing life-writing project. The phenomenon of virality has been explored, aiming at casting light on the affordances that facilitate synergies among significant social and political actors on the global stage. Despite slacktivism critics and those who deem such viral trends as passing fads, opportunist neoliberal acts, or leading nowhere really, the potential of the Web 2.0 and subsequent technological advances has notably been hailed by many other scholars and activists alike. This book does not offer a completely positive view of the digital, nor does it detract from its value. It simply states the obvious possibilities that the combination of both the online and the offline life-writing processes may offer. It opens the door to future explorations in novel forms of narrating the self, paving the way for other activists who wish to raise their voices in an increasingly "less mediated manner" (Martínez García 2017b, 133).

What's in a Name? Benefits and Pitfalls of Labeling and Tagging

The book has tried to address the following questions: What are the mechanisms by which these young girls and women suddenly become celebrities and are known by just their first name? In what Paul Frosh describes as the "incantation of the name" (2018, 20r), "tagged beings" (2018, 21a) are not just recipients of external attention, but creators and "produsers" (Bruns 2008) of that very tag. In fact, as Zizi Papacharissi has pointed out, "tagging both categorizes the performance and makes it accessible to wider audiences. It thus affords performative statements of the self greater visibility, effectively eponymizing them" (2012, 2000). How is it that so many other girls and women do not achieve this level of media attention and fall out of the public eye or their story is not even heard? How many "levels of mediation" (Douglas and Poletti 2016, 227) do these life-writing projects traverse before they reach the light? How intertwined are these first-person witness accounts with larger histories of suffering in co-constructed testimony (Gilmore 2017b, 307)? Though there is no easy answer to any of these questions, each of the previous chapters has attempted to underscore the multiplicity of approaches to life writing and mediation these young women take, showcasing relevant trends in twenty-first-century life writing.

Just as Malala Yousafzai (Chapter 2) stands for Pashtun girls, Hyeonseo Lee (Chapter 3) and Yeonmi Park (Chapter 4) for North Korean girls—the latter trafficked girls in China more specifically, Bana Alabed (Chapter 5) and Nujeen Mustafa (Chapter 6) for Syrian girls—the latter for Kurdish girls more specifically, Nadia Murad's (Chapter 7) activism has made her a global media icon, the emblem of a fight, namely standing for Yazidi girls enslaved by ISIS. These six young women activists do not need an introduction but tend to be known on a first-name basis as standing for the human rights they defend, the values they uphold. Their faces have, moreover, become symbolic for the social movements they have each engendered—global education for girls, North Korean rights, trafficked women rights, refugee rights, disabled rights, Yazidi rights. The recognition that stems from the visual realm expands into corporate value—Malala Fund and Nadia's Initiative are clear examples, both taking the first name of the main cofounder. Entering the public sphere as girls, they grow up as individuals and as collective selves.

Young Women Activists' Life-Writing Discursive Strategies

This book has presented a wide array of young women's life-writing projects where the deployment of "strategic narrative empathy" (Keen 2016) can be assessed. Together with a narrating "I" that collectivizes suffering (Smith and Watson 2010, 133), these girls are shown to employ various other rhetorical strategies in order to make their message stronger and more durable. Thus, their testimonial accounts are ripe with emotions that sway the reader/audience and may in turn move them to action (Keen 2008, 483). They appeal to universal emotions and experiences, as part of what Suzanne Keen calls "broadcast strategic empathy" (2016, 22). At the same time, the identity they create in their life writing is necessarily removed from readers/audiences, be that due to geographical, sociocultural, and/or political distance. This "ethnic" or "other" "I" utilizes, from the standpoint of the author, intentional "ambassadorial strategic empathy" (Keen 2016, 20). Nevertheless, unlike other humanitarian narratives, these texts do not simply ask for pity. Rather, their intent is to provoke ethical engagement with the cause they relay, removing potential obstacles in understanding the plight of others. Human rights life writing thus attests to the "paradox at the heart of human rights discourse and practice: the uneasy enfolding of the universal in the ethnic particular" (Smith 2006, 134). In this way, "the 'I' and the 'we' fluctuate and stand in dynamic tension" (Martínez García 2019a, 206). It is a productive kind of tension, out of which life writers emerge as survivors.

From Victim Girls to Activist Women

This book has brought together some current and influential human rights icons across the globe to shed light on their mechanisms of self-presentation, such as their strategic use of English as a rights lingua franca, their deployment of online/offline methods, and their resorting to empathy to generate concern (Martínez García 2016, 2017a, b, 2018, 2019a, b, 2020). In so doing, young women activists from the Global South appropriate the constructs underpinning self-representation in the Global North as a "significant gesture of resistance" (Moore-Gilbert 2009, 15). By writing themselves, they right the wrongs committed against them and regain, as empowered survivors, the agency that victimhood may have taken away from them. They exercise this life-writing agency in their projects, which may be seen in how their activist campaigns take shape.

Several characteristics connect the six activists and core chapters of this volume (Chapters 2–6). They all make use of social media as part of their activist life-writing projects, even if unevenly. Their memoirs have all been co-authored, but not all co-authors are acknowledged—some remain ghostwriters in near anonymity. By contrast, famous journalist Christina Lamb was not only co-author to one, but to two of the activists: Malala Yousafzai and Nujeen Mustafa. Could geopolitical stakes and age be factors? Lamb had experience reporting from war zones, these two young women are the only two teenage authors out of the six. Major international publishers act as mediators and disseminators, with their added marketability: Penguin and William Collins behind more than one.

Half of them are TED speakers: Hyeonseo Lee, Yeonmi Park, Nujeen Mustafa—three activists share the fact that they speak for refugee rights, a pressing matter in contemporary times. Though they all write themselves as activists, thereby asserting the agency to do so and arguably transgressing patriarchal norms, only two have been hailed as feminist icons—Malala and Yeonmi—and only two have claimed to have been trafficked: Yeonmi and Nadia (and to a lesser extent Hyeonseo and Nujeen).

A crucial mediator is the United Nations, after all the organization that shaped the Universal Declaration of Human Rights and subsequent documents and whose values they all strive to uphold. The six young women have all spoken at the United Nations: Malala Yousafzai at the Youth Assembly (United Nations 2013), Security Council (Malo 2016), and General Assembly (United Nations 2017a); Hyeonseo Lee at the UNSC (Lee 2014); Yeonmi Park at UNHCR (UN Watch 2015); Bana Alabed at the UN headquarters (United Nations 2017b); Nujeen Mustafa (United Nations 2019) and Nadia Murad at UNSC (Nichols 2015). Despite their presence at UN events, only two have held UN roles: Malala as UN Messenger of Peace (United Nations 2017a) and Nadia as UNODC Goodwill Ambassador (UNODC 2016). It is precisely these two activists who have also received the Nobel Peace Prize. The repercussions of collaborating with UN agencies do matter for human rights activists to be perceived as vital voices in the global arena.

At a time of human rights anniversaries, these six young women's life-writing projects become timely reads. References to the Universal Declaration of Human Rights (UDHR) (United Nations 1948), though usually indirect, without specifying the articles they mention, are a feature of human rights activism and activists' life writing. As a general "frame of reference" (Schaffer and Smith 2004, 116), the rights enshrined in the Declaration are those by which victims turned survivors wish states and other actors involved in the violence and injustice they suffered to be bound to. Yet, as opposed to human rights experts, lawyers, and advocates, by focusing on their personal experience they avoid facts and data, among which is the actual wording of each of the UDHR articles. Important dates are the 70th anniversary of the UDHR (OHCHR 2018) and the 30th anniversary of the Convention on the Rights of the Child (CRC) (United Nations 1989) (OHCHR 2019), both anniversaries that, even if the young women do not engage with, the print and media industry surrounding them do. As testimonial texts enter the public sphere, audiences around the world are likely to see them and read them in light of these two documents, as life-writing activists, after all, fight for access to what they refer to as universal claims to human rights on the basis of being human beings, and suffering as they were children makes them expect that the rights expounded in the CRC should be legally binding throughout the world, in a universal call for justice. In a kind of symbiotic relationship, life-writing projects such as the ones discussed in this volume raise awareness about the UDHR and related documents and institutions, while said institutions invite the survivors to speak and/or testify on various occasions. This is something all the activists in this book share—their testimony has been backed up and advanced, disseminated further, by being complicit in United Nations events and other major transnational organizations.

It would be oversimplifying to welcome all rights narratives as ethically unproblematic. Leigh Gilmore (2017a) warns against "an ethics built on sympathy" (127), while Gillian Whitlock (2007) explains how the ethics of testimony "are always open to question" (85). Sidonie Smith and Julia Watson (2010) remind readers that, when empathy fails, it forecloses the possibility of an "ethic of responsibility" connecting witness and audience (221). Overall, the ambivalence these testimonies present is in no way intended to leave readers/audiences passively waiting for answers. It is, predictably, a serious challenge to one-sided readings of pressing import that should benefit from our ethical work as readers, researchers, and academics, to inform ourselves and perhaps then inform others. I believe studying these life-writing projects can help guide such a self-reflective process. My reading is not meant to preclude or obscure other readings. On the contrary, I want to end on a positive note, inviting my colleagues to participate in the lively debate of where the interdisciplinary field of human rights activism, gender studies, and life writing in the twenty-first century is taking us.

Works Cited

Bruns, Axel. 2008. *Blogs, Wikipedia, Second Life, and Beyond: From Production to Produsage*. New York: Peter Lang.

Douglas, Kate, and Anna Poletti. 2016. *Life Narratives and Youth Culture: Representation, Agency and Participation*. London: Palgrave Macmillan.

Frosh, Paul. 2018. *The Poetics of Digital Media*. Cambridge, UK: Polity Press.

Gilmore, Leigh. 2017a. *Tainted Witness: Why We Doubt What Women Say About Their Lives*. New York: Columbia University Press.

———. 2017b. Testimony. *a/b: Auto/Biography Studies* 32 (2): 307–309.

Keen, Suzanne. 2008. Strategic Empathizing: Techniques of Bounded, Ambassadorial, and Broadcast Narrative Empathy. *Deutsche Vierteljahrsschrift für Literaturwissenchaft und Geistesgeschichte* 82 (3): 477–493.

———. 2016. Life Writing and the Empathetic Circle. *Concentric: Literary and Cultural Studies* 42 (2): 9–26.

Lee, Hyeonseo. 2014. Hyeonseo Lee Speaks at UN Security Council New York. *Hyeonseo Lee*, 11 April. http://www.hyeonseo-lee.com/eng/hyeonseo-lee-speeks-at-un-security-council-new-york_28966.shtml. Accessed 13 March 2020.

Malo, Sebastien. 2016. End Violence in Myanmar, Nobel Laureates Urge U.N. Security Council. *Reuters*, 29 December. https://www.reuters.com/article/us-myanmar-rohingya-letter-idUSKBN14I1UB. Accessed 13 March 2020.

Martínez García, Ana Belén. 2016. Narrative Emotions and Human Rights Life Writing. In *On the Move: Glancing Backwards to Build a Future in English Studies*, ed. Aitor Ibarrola-Armendariz and Jon Ortiz de Urbina Arruabarrena, 127–132. Bilbao: University of Deusto.

———. 2017a. Unearthing the Past: Bringing Ideological Indoctrination to Light in North Korean Girls' Memoirs. *a/b: Auto/Biography Studies* 32 (3): 587–602.

———. 2017b. Bana Alabed: Using Twitter to Draw Attention to Human Rights Violations. *Prose Studies: History, Theory, Criticism* 39 (2–3): 132–149.

———. 2018. TED Talks as Life Writing: Online and Offline Activism. *Life Writing* 15 (4): 487–503.

———. 2019a. Construction and Collaboration in Life-Writing Projects: Malala Yousafzai's Activist 'I'. *Journal of Writing in Creative Practice* 12 (1–2): 201–217.

———. 2019b. Denouncing Human Trafficking in China: North Korean Women's Memoirs as Evidence. *State Crime Journal* 8 (1): 59–79.

———. 2020. Women Activists' Strategies of Online Self-Presentation. *AI & Society: Journal of Knowledge, Culture and Communication*. Special Issue on Iteration as Persuasion in a Digital World. Forthcoming.

Moore-Gilbert, Bart. 2009. *Postcolonial Life-Writing: Culture, Politics and Self-Representation*. Abingdon: Routledge.

Nichols, Michelle. 2015. Yazidi Woman Begs U.N. Security Council to Wipe Out Islamic State. *Reuters*, 16 December. https://www.reuters.com/article/islamic-state-un/yazidi-woman-begs-u-n-security-council-to-wipe-out-islamic-state-idINKBN0TZ33B20151216. Accessed 13 March 2020.

Office of the United Nations High Commissioner for Human Rights (OHCHR). 2018. 70th Anniversary of the Universal Declaration of Human Rights. *OHCHR*, 6 December. https://www.ohchr.org/EN/NewsEvents/Pages/DisplayNews.aspx. Accessed 13 March 2020.

———. 2019. Celebrating 30 Years of the Convention on the Rights of the Child. *OHCHR*, 20 November. https://www.ohchr.org/EN/HRBodies/CRC/Pages/CRC30.aspx. Accessed 13 March 2020.

Papacharissi, Zizi. 2012. Without You, I'm Nothing: Performances of the Self on Twitter. *International Journal of Communication* 6: 1989–2006.

Schaffer, Kay, and Sidonie Smith. 2004. *Human Rights and Narrated Lives: The Ethics of Recognition*. New York: Palgrave.

Smith, Sidonie. 2006. Narratives and Rights: *Zlata's Diary* and the Circulation of Stories of Suffering Ethnicity. *WSQ: Women's Studies Quarterly* 34 (1–2): 133–152.
Smith, Sidonie, and Julia Watson. 2010. *Reading Autobiography: A Guide for Interpreting Life Narratives*, 2nd ed. Minneapolis: Minnesota University Press.
UN Watch. 2015. 21-Year-Old North Korean Survivor Addresses UN Debate. *UN Watch*, 21 September. https://unwatch.org/21-year-old-north-korean-survivor-addresses-un-debate/. Accessed 13 March 2020.
United Nations. 1948. Universal Declaration of Human Rights. https://undocs.org/A/RES/217(III). Accessed 13 March 2020.
———. 1989. Convention on the Rights of the Child. *United Nations Treaty Collection*. https://treaties.un.org/doc/Publication/MTDSG/Volume%20I/Chapter%20IV/IV-11.en.pdf. Accessed 13 March 2020.
———. 2013. Malala Yousafzai Addresses United Nations Youth Assembly. *YouTube*, 13 July. https://www.youtube.com/watch?v=3rNhZu3ttIU. Accessed 12 March 2020.
———. 2017a. Malala Yousafzai Designated Youngest-Ever UN Messenger of Peace. *Sustainable Development Goals*, 10 April. https://www.un.org/sustainabledevelopment/blog/2017/04/malala-yousafzai-designated-youngest-ever-un-messenger-of-peace/. Accessed 13 March 2020.
——— (@UN). 2017b. "I want to tell the world about the children in war" - @AlabedBana who tweeted her daily experiences from Syria was at UN to deliver this msg. *Twitter*, 7 October. https://twitter.com/UN/status/916695639072808962. Accessed 13 March 2020.
———. 2019. 'You Can and Should Do More' to Include People with Disabilities, Wheelchair-Bound Syrian Advocate Tells Security Council in Searing Speech. *UN News*, 24 April. https://news.un.org/en/story/2019/04/1037291. Accessed 13 March 2020.
United Nations Office on Drugs and Crime (UNODC). 2016. Human Trafficking Survivor Nadia Murad Named UNODC Goodwill Ambassador. *UNODC*, 16 September. https://www.unodc.org/unodc/en/frontpage/2016/September/human-trafficking-survivor-nadia-murad-named-unodc-goodwill-ambassador.html. Accessed 13 March 2020.
Whitlock, Gillian. 2007. *Soft Weapons: Autobiography in Transit*. Chicago: University of Chicago Press.

Index

A. B. Martínez García, *New Forms of Self-Narration*, Palgrave Studies in Life Writing, https://doi.org/10.1007/978-3-030-46420-2

R

S